DATE			
	.		

APR   1996

BAKER & TAYLOR

MUSIC of the

ANCIENT NEAR EAST

CLAIRE C. J. POLIN

GREENWOOD PRESS, PUBLISHERS
WESTPORT, CONNECTICUT

Library of Congress Cataloging in Publication Data

Polin, Claire C   J
    Music of the ancient Near East.

    Reprint of the ed. published by Vantage Press, New
York.
    "Musical examples": p.
    Bibliography: p.
    1. Music--History and criticism--Ancient. 2. Music
--Asia Minor. 3. Music--Egypt. 4. Musical instru-
ments--Asia Minor. 5. Musical instruments--Egypt.
I. Title.
[ML162.P7 1974]   780'.93   73-20879
ISBN 0-8371-5796-X

Originally published in 1954 by Vantage Press, Inc.,
New York

Reprinted with the permission of Claire C. J. Polin.

Reprinted in 1974 by Greenwood Press,
a division of Congressional Information Service, Inc.
51 Riverside Avenue, Westport, Connecticut 06880

Library of Congress catalog card number 73-20879
ISBN 0-8371-5796-X

Printed in the United States of America.

10 9 8 7 6 5 4 3

*In dedicating this book to the teachers and students
of Gratz College, Philadelphia, I hope to repay
a debt of long standing.*

FOREWORD

Claire Polin, in this book on the antiquity of musical instruments, makes a strong claim for the origin of some of our most familiar instruments in the ancient Semitic world of the Near East. I suppose that most of us, remembering Homer and the Greek singers, think of the harp and the flute as characteristically Greek in the heroic epoch of the late Bronze Age. But, for those who have seen the famed collection of treasures from the royal tombs at Ur of the Chaldees, now in the University Museum and in the British Museum, there can be no doubt that these instruments, in sophisticated forms, were already a part of everyday life at the very dawn of civilized living nearly fifteen hundred years before the fall of Troy.

When the biblical genealogies claim one Jubal as "the father of all such as handle the lyre and pipe," naming him as a descendant of Adam, they are reflecting the long heritage of music in the biblical world which is now confirmed by archaeological discoveries throughout the Near East. It is this fact of the antiquity of song, and of many of the kinds of instruments now making up our symphony orchestras, which this book re-emphasizes for those readers who are interested not only in the technical history of musical instruments, but in the whole story of man, and it is this fact which impresses all of us who are archaeologists rather than musicians. Just as a fragmentary script describing the beliefs of the ancients often gives us an intimate glimpse at the individual lives of long forgotten people, so the concrete proof of highly developed musical instruments and the musical knowledge they represent brings to us a vivid sense of the daily life and thought of people, much like ourselves, who lived five thousand years ago.

One of the exciting things about archaeology is that we never really find the beginning. We can say only that at some given time a thing or an idea is there. But whether it is there or somewhere else much earlier remains to be seen. In the following story of ancient musical instruments, you will see that curiously modern forms appear in astonishingly early times. But, are they inventions of Sumerian or Semitic speaking peoples, or are they gifts of some earlier, as yet entirely unknown, people of a world not yet discovered? Larger and more effective telescopes steadily expand the universe. The diggers in their relatively short history have in the same way steadily expanded the history of men. There is no reason at all to believe that we have certainly found the beginning of any one idea.

I hope in reading this you will discover that the joy of music is an age-old heritage of man and also that archaeology applied to music gives us one more proof of familiar chords in human nature recurring like a musical theme throughout the ages.

FROELICH RAINEY

The University Museum
Philadelphia

PREFACE

"The orbit of Western music has passed beyond the
point furthest from Oriental music, and in its cyclic
course is again approaching regions we thought we had
left for good. With the illusion of ever-flowing progress
broken, our musicians have begun to realize that once
more, they themselves are engaged in the ceaseless
battle for melody and rhythm that their ancestors
fought for in the rise of music in Asia and Europe."
—CURT SACHS, *The Rise of Music in the
Ancient World, East and West.*

THIS BOOK REPRESENTS AN ATTEMPT TO RECAPTURE THE
compositional ideas of the ancient world. For musicians
today, abstract as well as programmatic types of early
music still furnish untapped springs of compositional pos-
sibilities. If we apply Spengler's theory concerning the
cyclic quality of history to art, we discover that endless
seeking and striving for self-expression have led the composer throughout the ages to cast off the limitations of his
day and to discover newer outlets, which in turn become
a limiting factor for the next generation. So, continuous
evolution has brought the contemporary composer to a
point of return. His quest for freedom of expression has

caused him to discard the rules of harmony, traditional rhythms, melodic limitations, even of the twelve-tone system, and to seek a new means of expression. Some have found it in freedom from harmonic structure, others in quarter tones and microtones. Oriental music becomes their precedent, and a need for a deeper knowledge of its inception and development becomes obvious. Conversely, in order to comprehend fully the essence of any phase of modern living and thought, it is necessary not only to experience it in its present state, but to study its genesis and its flowering growth. Thus, we cannot view any period of past culture with contempt, lest by doing so we sever our present world from its very foundations. As life is the apex of a pyramid of past experiences, so art of the present day is a cultural agglutination of past forms of expression.

The highest expressions of ancient art have never been eclipsed. Such masterpieces as the bust of Nefretiti, the Sumerian royal tomb jewelry and pottery, the "Song of the Harper," and the "Song of Songs" stand unsurpassed today. Of our many heritages, the Semitic cradle of civilization had one of the strongest influences on world thought and development. Approximately one half of humanity's historic span on earth was influenced by Mesopotamia. Three thousand years of world history had been recorded there even before its cultural offshoots, Persia, Syria, Palestine, eventually influenced the world in all directions, from India to America.

In its ascendancy, the eastern end of the Mediterranean formed a cultural bloc for easy interchange of aesthetic and instrumental techniques. The Egyptians developed columnar architecture at an early period in history and may possibly have passed this on to Asia, the Greek pen-

insula, Rome, and finally Europe. Such things characteristically Egyptian as the pyramids, sphinxes, and obelisks,
have left an indelible imprint on the history of architecture. The influence of Egyptian literature was mentioned
by Herodotus, the father of Greek history, in the fifth
century B.C., while Alexandria, as a center of culture,
created a fusion of Greek and Egyptian thought.

The Near East has given us the sciences, particularly
astronomy, mathematics, and the sexagesimal system of
counting. It undoubtedly influenced the Hebrew Bible
and other classics, and gave to the world one of the greatest governmental constitutions, the Code of Hammurabi.
It also developed to a high degree a system of taxation,
commercial transactions, both inter- and intra-urban, and
provided a system of record keeping to insure the just and
unfailing collection of taxes.

The culture of the Hebrews is so much a part of our
modern daily life that we do not separate in recognition
the customs of Hebrew origin from other sources. Most
common names (John, Mary, Susan, etc.) are of Hebrew
origin. The three great Western religions stem from monotheism, a Hebrew contribution to religion. To a large extent, the ethical concepts of Europe are based on the
Bible, and many everyday English idioms, such as "the
skin of one's teeth," "ivory tower," and "sour grapes"
are taken directly from the Bible. As literature, the Bible
still influences creativeness, and is reflected in Negro spir-
ituals, in the themes used in operas, paintings, modern
literature, political speeches, the use of the seven-day week,
the day of rest, the anointing of kings, and so forth.

The purpose of this book, in brief, is to demonstrate
the place of music in the life of the ancient Semitic cul-

tures, and to investigate the types of music these people developed through a study of their instruments and literary texts set to music.

The music of the most ancient nations can be studied most effectively through literary as well as non-literary sources. In Egypt, the position that music occupied can be surmised by studying the documents and actual remains of ancient instruments. The foremost references concerning Palestine are the paintings at Beni Hasan, the mention of instruments in the Bible, literary texts which were set to music, and dances. In other countries, documentary and archaeological references are a great aid.

Source materials may be divided into the following categories:

a) *Literary sources:* The Hebrew Bible, Greek and Latin classic authors, cuneiform writings, philological material available in Babylonian and Assyrian, a study of the foremost historic languages of the Middle East, and Egyptian inscriptions.

b) *Non-literary sources:* Archaeological discoveries of instruments and their reconstruction, and examples concerning music in glyptic art. Dividing art into architectural and movable units, we find examples of the life of early peoples in the former category by observing their temples, dwellings, fortifications, streets, and tombs. The latter group is usually divided again into fine arts (aesthetic) and artifacts (utilitarian). In Palestine, where there was a dearth of fine art, ceramics yield information; in Mesopotamia and Egypt, so much fine art exists, that artifacts are generally ignored. Cylinder seals provide one of the best sources for revealing forms of culture. Reliefs, statues, paintings, metal works, miniature models, as well as coins from the seventh century B.C. onward, serve to enlighten the student of ancient life.

I wish to acknowledge my gratitude to those persons who have been of inestimable aid to me in writing this work; notably, Dr. Samuel N. Kramer of the University of Pennsylvania, Dr. Cyrus Gordon of Dropsie College and of Princeton University, and Dr. Eric Werner of the Hebrew Union College at Cincinnati, for their valuable suggestions concerning the study of the Sumerian epics and the theory of musical rhythm, the survey of Egyptian instruments and art objects, and the study of temple songs and instruments, respectively. I am also greatly indebted to Mrs. Evelyn Quick of the Philadelphia Conservatory of Music for her constant interest and well-directed help throughout the writing of this book. Also, I wish to express gratitude to Dr. Rudolf Anthès, Mr. Henry Fischer, and to the various members of the staff of the University Museum in Philadelphia, for placing within my reach many of the sources of material which make up this book; to Mr. Leon N. Cohanne for his splendid illustrations and many artistic suggestions; to Mr. Merle S. Schaff, without whose constructive criticism this book would probably not have been written; and to the many others who were of aid. To the Metropolitan Museum in New York, the University Museum in Philadelphia, and the Chicago Oriental Institute, I am indebted for permission to use the photographic illustrations included herein.

Philadelphia, Pennsylvania
June, 1953   C. C. J. P.

CONTENTS

		Page
Foreword		V
Preface		VII
List of Illustrations		XIV
Introduction		XVII
Chapter	I MESOPOTAMIA	1
	II EGYPT	22
	III PALESTINE	49
	IV ARABIA	77
	V ASSYRIA	86
	VI PHOENICIA	95
	VII SYRIA	99
	VIII ABYSSINIA	103
Conclusion		108
Appendices		113
	A. Theoretical Notation of a Sumerian Hymn	113
	B. Egyptian Poetry	115
	C. Chart of Comparative Cantillations	119
	D. Comparative Scales and Meters	121
	E. Musical Examples	123
Bibliography		129
Index		135

LIST OF ILLUSTRATIONS

HALF-TONE PLATES AND DRAWINGS OF MUSICAL INSTRUMENTS

MESOPOTAMIA

I   Harp from Ur
II   Gilgamesh Panels from
      Ur Harp
III Concussion Sticks
IV Double Oboe from Ur
V   Reconstruction of
      Double Oboe

VI   Figurine Playing
      Double Oboe
VII Silver Lyre
VIII Lute
IX   Horizontal Harp or
      Dulcimer
X   Cithara

EGYPT

XI   Chamber Orchestra from Theban Wall Painting
XII Chamber Orchestra from a Tomb Wall Painting
XIII Twin-Clarinet

PALESTINE

XIV   V-Notched Flute
XV   Flageolet
XVI   Bagpipe
XVII Hydraulis

XVIII Ram's Horn (Shofar)
XIX   Oliphant
XX   Lyre from a Wall
       Painting

ARABIA

XXI   Tambourine
XXII   Wooden Horn
XXIII Turkish Lute

XXIV Notched Lute
XXV   Kemângeh-a-Gûz
XXVI Rebâb

SYRIA

XXVII Gourd Trumpet

xiv

ABYSSINIA

XXVIII Kettledrum

LINE DRAWINGS IN THE TEXT

A.	Zulu Bow	xix
B.	Prehistoric Bone Whistle	xix
C.	Sumerian Drum (Balaggu)	15
D.	Naos Sistrum	37
E.	Bullroarer	37
F.	Egyptian Musicians (Trumpet and Flute)	40
G.	Egyptian Stringed Instruments	43
H.	Angle Harp	44
I.	Lyres on Hebrew Coins	48
J.	Arabian Bagpipe	80
K.	Kanoon or Zither	82
L.	Kessar	82
M.	Assyrian Cymbals	90
N.	Clay Flute	91
O.	Assyrian Single Pipe	91
P.	Horizontal Harp	92
Q.	Assyrian Lyre	92
R.	Phoenician Instruments (Psaltery, Timbrel, Double Pipes)	97
S.	Syrian Drum	101
T.	Abyssinian Trumpet	105
U.	Abyssinian Fiddle and Crescent Bow	105
V.	Standing Lyre	106
W.	Bow-Shaped Lyre	106

Mesopotamia

I. HARP
from Ur of the
Chaldees, partly
reconstructed.
(*Courtesy University
Museum*)

II. PANELS
of ivory inlay, depicting
four sections of the Gilgamesh
Epic on the front of the
Harp from Ur.
(*Courtesy University Museum*)

Mesopotamia

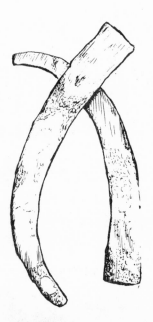

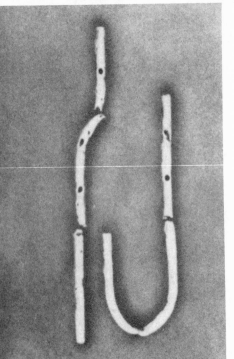

III. CONCUSSION-STICKS
used by a dancer, excavated
at Fara near the Euphrates,
dating circa 2500 B. C.
(Courtesy University Museum)

IV. DOUBLE OBOE
excavated from the Royal
Cemetery near Ur, circa
2800 B. C.
(Courtesy University Museum)

Mesopotamia

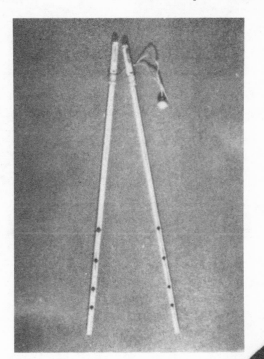

V. DOUBLE OBOE
from Ur, reconstructed by
Jesse-Phillips Robertson.
(*Courtesy University Museum*)

VI. DOUBLE OBOE
held by a terra cotta
figurine, found at Nippur
of the First Babylonian
Dynasty.
(*Courtesy University Museum*)

Mesopotamia

VII. SILVER LYRE
with Stag, excavated
from the Death Pit,
circa 3000 B. C.
*(Courtesy University
Museum)*

VIII. LUTE
depicted on a clay
plaque, played
by a shepherd
with dogs.

Mesopotamia

IX. DULCIMER
or horizontal harp,
depicted on a clay plaque,
played by a man while
marching.

X. CITHARA
played by a winged Eros.
Of much later origin,
it is executed in classical
style.

Egypt

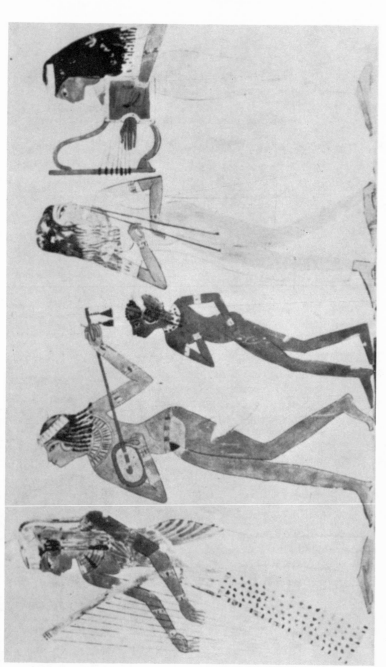

XI. **CHAMBER ORCHESTRA** of the Eighteenth Dynasty, from a Theban wall-painting depicting banquet musicians performing on *harp, lute, double oboe,* and *lyre.*
(*Courtesy Davies and Gardiner, "Ancient Egyptian Paintings," Oriental Institute*)

Egypt

XII. ORCHESTRA

consisting of *double oboe* player, singers and dancers, from a wall-painting on the tomb of Thuthmosis IV or Amenophis II.
(Courtesy Metropolitan Museum of Art)

XIII. TWIN CLARINET,

called *Zummâra Settawia*, of Moroccan cane, believed to be of ancient Egyptian origin.

Palestine

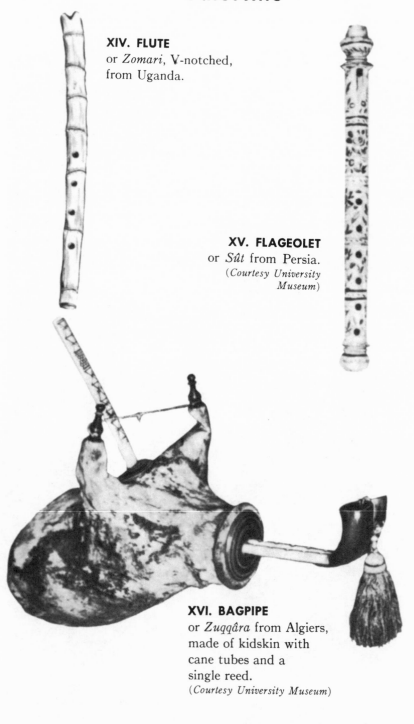

XIV. FLUTE
or *Zomari*, V-notched,
from Uganda.

XV. FLAGEOLET
or *Sût* from Persia.
(*Courtesy University
Museum*)

XVI. BAGPIPE
or *Zuqqâra* from Algiers,
made of kidskin with
cane tubes and a
single reed.
(*Courtesy University Museum*)

XVII. HYDRAULIS
of bronze from Pompeii
or Herculaneum.
(Courtesy University Museum)

Palestine

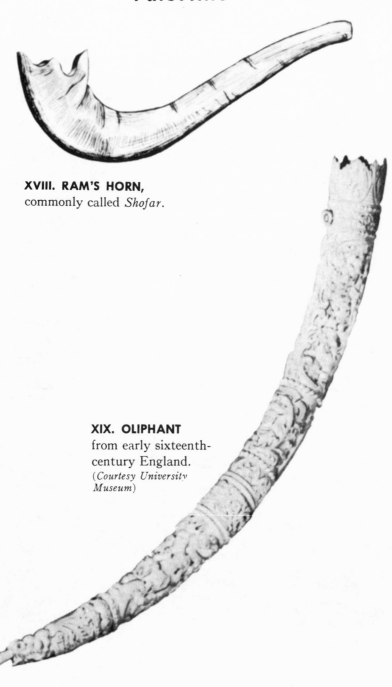

XVIII. RAM'S HORN,
commonly called *Shofar*.

XIX. OLIPHANT
from early sixteenth-
century England.
(*Courtesy University
Museum*)

Palestine

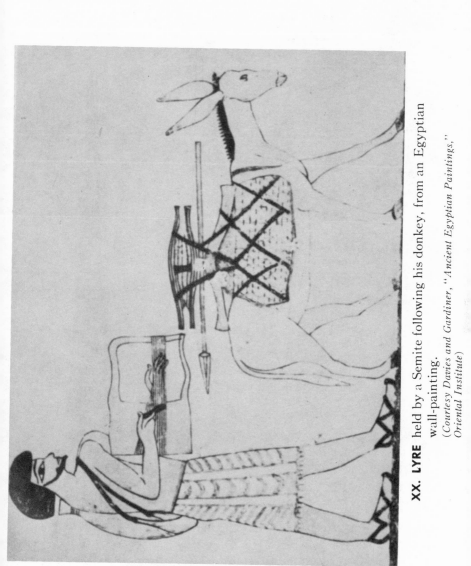

XX. LYRE held by a Semite following his donkey, from an Egyptian wall-painting.

(*Courtesy Davies and Gardiner, "Ancient Egyptian Paintings," Oriental Institute*)

Arabia

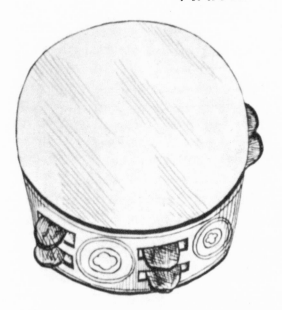

XXI. TAMBOURINE
or *Tar* from Morocco,
with disk jigglers and
membrane top.

XXII. HORN
or *Al Gaita* from Nigeria,
made of conically bored
wood.
(*Courtesy University Museum*)

Arabia

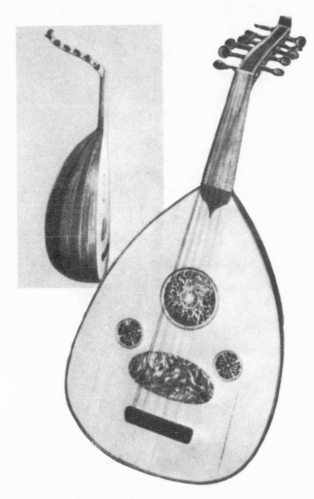

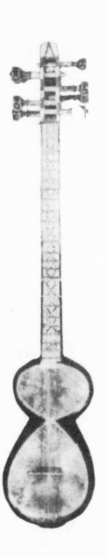

XXIII. LUTE,
called *Al'ud*, an eleven-
stringed Turkish instrument
with finely carved rosettes.
(*Courtesy University Museum*)

XXIV. LUTE,
or *Tar*, from Tiflis, a notched
instrument with movable
frets.
(*Courtesy University Museum*)

Arabia

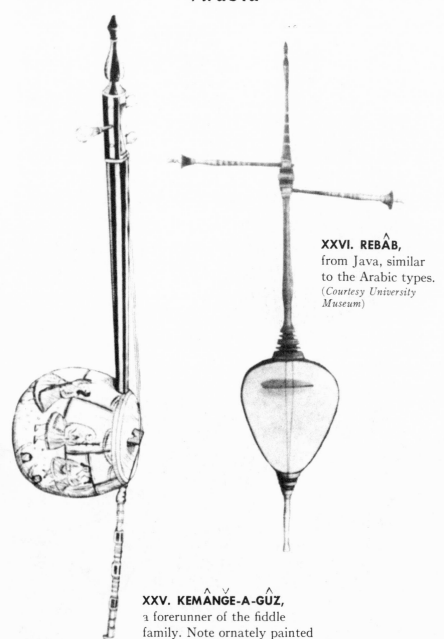

XXVI. REBÂB,
from Java, similar
to the Arabic types.
*(Courtesy University
Museum)*

XXV. KEMÂNGĔ-A-GÛZ,
a forerunner of the fiddle
family. Note ornately painted
cocoanut resonator.

Syria

XXVII. TRUMPET,
made of a polyglobular
gourd, from Damascus.
(*Courtesy University
Museum*)

Abyssinia

XXVIII. KETTLEDRUM,
or Abyssinian
Nagârit, laced with
twisted rawhide
thongs.
(*Courtesy University
Museum*)

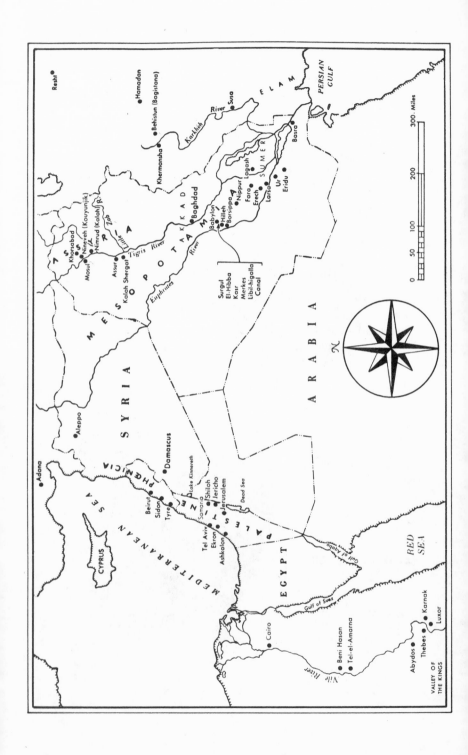

INTRODUCTION

MUSIC HAS ALWAYS BEEN AN INNATE EXPRESSION OF MAN, as is evidenced by the common acceptance of singing as being the daughter of speech. Human speech developed through three stages: prose talk, poetry, and song. The purpose of poetry, or chanting, led to song. The rise and fall of pitches caused chants to develop definite tonal structures. As speech, when solemn or impassioned, passes into chanting, so chanting, at regular intervals, becomes singing. Chants and all early vocalizations were not bound by definite pitch.[1] The purpose of song was to convey poetic

---

1 Some examples of barbarian chants may be found in the Australian monotonous chants before fights or funerals, and in North America hunting chants. Among nations at a slightly higher stage of culture, regular meter appears: i.e., ancient Vedic hymns. For further discussion, see Taylor, *Anthropology,* chapters on music and dance.

ideas, to give a hypnotic trance to the sick, to awaken the dancer's muscles, or to hearten the fighting man.[2]

Primitive song was understood by all men. No *personal* idiom existed, for singing was the reflection of the life of the whole tribe; its soul was everyone's soul.[3] Singing was frequently connected with the pantomime dance. Various rhythmic impulses which we observe as psychological normalities in children may be said to have been the earliest musical expressions in the childhood of civilization. War calls, yodeling, wild clapping, rhythmic jumping and dancing, and humming formed an integral part of the tribal life of savages. Later on, humming developed into a type of polyphony. Octaves were unavoidable because of both sexes singing together. Gradually, fifths and fourths crept in, and we discover melodies with an occasional drone or monotone accompaniment. When intervals became known to the early Mesopotamians and Chinese, they were used to characterize the seasons of the year: the octave represented summer; the fifth, winter; the

---

2 One of the most distinctive features of early chant was that musically it was logogenic, or word-born (notes used as vehicles for words), while true song which developed later was essentially pathogenic, having emotions and melodic lines take precedence over the words. See Sachs, *The Rise of Music in the Ancient World, East and West.*

3 Sachs, in *The Rise of Music in the Ancient World, East and West,* has an unusual discussion on the combination of poetry and song. He says, in essence, that there was no primeval unity of singing and poetry which derived melodies from natural speech tones of words. Poetry, in its purest sense, leads the melody in words away from conventional speech. Art denaturalizes nature in order to raise it to a higher level. Poets disfigure speech by replacing free expressive rhythms of spoken phrases with patterns of long and short, strong and light—"they replace common words by uncommon words, and rearrange grammar." Singers in their turn avoid the vague tones of a spoken word on one note, and turn to a series of uniform steps between two and three notes on a medium level.

fourth, autumn; and the unison, spring. Every sound, every accent in early music had a specific meaning.

The earliest instruments probably stemmed from the rattle, the drum, and the whistle. The earliest records we have of musical instruments are of those belonging to paleolithic man, such as a flute made of reindeer's horn in the Stone Age,[4] various open or skin-covered hollow logs used as drums, and, in the Bronze Age, metal horns. Besides these, there probably were gongs, cymbals, hunting whis-

FIGURE A. ZULU BOW

FIGURE B. PREHISTORIC BONE WHISTLE
(*Arrow Points to Artificial Hole*)

---

4 In Engel, *Musical Instruments,* we find the following description: "Exhumed in France, it was used as a whistle for hunting animals. It is a first digital phalanx of a ruminant, drilled to a certain depth by a smooth cylindrical bore on its lower surface near the expanded upper articulation. On applying it to the lower lip and blowing into it, a shrill sound is yielded." (See Figure B.)

tles, and hollow trees which resounded when blown. Of this period, Engel in his *Musical Instruments* also mentions a stag horn with three fingerholes, which was blown at the open end like a flûte-à-bec, and which yielded distinct tones.

Stringed instruments developed somewhat later and were extremely popular. There is much mention made of them in early literature. In Egypt, as early as the Eighteenth Dynasty, mandolins, harps, lutes, and lyres were common. In the *Odyssey*, the avenging hero twangs the mighty bow, producing a musical tone. The Demara tribe of South Africa find pleasure in striking a taut bow-string with a small stick to produce a faint tone. The Zulus consider the bow a cowardly weapon, but use it in a novel fashion for music: the bow has a ring which is slid along to alter the tone, with a hollow gourd acting as resonator, or soundbox. (See Figure A.)

From instruments capable of producing only one sound but each having different pitches, developed the *scale*. The most primitive scales are the Natural (brought to man by the trumpet) and the Pentatonic. They have been used throughout the history of music.

In early times, the dance was inseparable from music. Dancing achieved full meaning in early civilization as an expression of all of life's acts: courting, war, peace, harvest, magic, religion. Among the Mandan Indians, when there was a dearth of buffaloes, they danced for weeks until they sighted a herd of animals. Among the Egyptians, Greeks, Romans, and Tibetans, the dance was used as a religious rite, frequently combined with acting. Some examples are bear dances, dog dances, Dionysian dances, and religious pantomimes. So narrow was the connecting thread between singing and arm or dance motions among the Egyptians, that their expression for "singing" was synonymous with "to play with the hand." The influence of women was strongly felt in shaping the structure of early music and dance. Perfect symmetry was an important feature of the feminine dance.[5]

---

5 Sachs, Curt, *World History of the Dance.*

MESOPOTAMIA:

GENESIS OF SEMITIC CULTURE

When the heaven above was not named,
And the sea beneath had no name,
Of Apsu primordial, their father,
And of tumultuous Tiamat, the all-mother,
The waters mingled in one.
The rush-beds were not fixed; the reed breaks were
  unseen,
When no god had been named, when no fate was
  appointed,
The gods they were created.

POEM OF CREATION[6]

BETWEEN TWO RIVERS, THE TIGRIS AND EUPHRATES, LIES
Mesopotamia, whose most ancient known cities are Lagash,
Babylon, and Ur. The culture of its inhabitants, from
most ancient times, was of a high level. They constructed
homes and temples of brick, and built their cities on artificial escarpments to forestall floods. They possessed numerous flocks and herds, irrigated their land by an im-
mense network of canals fed by the Euphrates, constructed
watering machines, worked copper and silver, and fashioned arms and metal. Sculpture was still crude and naïve,

---

6 Tablet No. 93014, British Museum, found at Assur and probably dating
  back to the first half of the second millennium B.C.

1

but their script showed great development, being no longer pictographic.

Plant life consisted of barley, starch, and wheat which grew wild, sesame, and in pre-Sargonic times (before 2500 B.C.), mention was made even of fig trees, pomegranates, dates, onions, and cucumbers. The fauna consisted of asses, cattle, sheep, goats, pigs, dogs, poultry, lions, bison, buffalo, deer, leopards, wild goats, antelopes, eagles, snakes, scorpions, and several varieties of fish. Bee culture was also quite common.

The people of Mesopotamia were of two origins. In the south, the Sumerians were of non-Semitic origin; in the north were the Akkadians, the early Syrian Semites. The earliest literature is recorded in Sumerian cuneiform, (*circa* 3000 B.C.), and consists mainly of economic, classical, and religious writings. The society was organized into small city-states, each of which excelled in a different craft. Ur, the city of Abraham, for example, excelled in metallurgic skill. The greatest Semitic figure was Sargon I (2500 B.C.), a military leader whose life story is replete with colorful legends and deeds. One of the most constructive leaders to follow was Gudea, who encouraged a revival of the arts. He built canals and temples, stimulated trade, and laid emphasis on a constructive life. We know this from extant texts of the period, which were presented in duplicate to insure veracity. The founder of Babylonian unity and law was Hammurabi. Under his skillful administration, Babylonian culture spread to Asia Minor.

Society at this time was divided into three classes: noblemen, commoners, and slaves. The cost of living was regulated by fixed price levels, and there was the equivalent of our G.I. Bill of Rights, as well as traffic regulations, and limited monogamy. Laws concerning marriage, divorce, inheritance, and women's rights were very rigid. Hospitality was a cardinal virtue, due to the precarious conditions which prevailed. The Hittites, who later contributed to the destruction of Babylon, first brought Asiatic culture to Europe. They contributed language, use of chariots, and use of horsepower to Europe, and by the time of the Minoan civilization in Crete, established sufficient prosperity for the prevalence of unwalled cities.

Sumerian-Akkadian culture left a deep imprint on subsequent civilizations. Its influence on the Mediterranean coast and Asia Minor was maintained from the time of Sargon's expeditions. Fourteen centuries later, we find references in the Tel-el-Amarna letters concerning the relations between Babylonia and Egypt. This culture left the world richer in methods of agriculture, skillful metallurgy, the phalanx form of battle tactics, and literary monuments on cylinder seals, chiefly concerning science and history. Mesopotamian ethical standards have been handed down through Hebrew as well as Egyptian sources. Extreme loyalty and fidelity unto death were outstanding traits mentioned in early epics (note that servants, guards, and animals are usually buried with the dying prince).

Mesopotamian art should be mentioned in connection with the influence it exerted on the world about. Early art-forms strove for permanence and reserve; we note the blocklike statues of impersonal rulers portraying no slightest gesture. The human element was thus excluded, no women or youth being represented. Ornamentation was strict and symmetrical. Only after the collapse of the

Babylonian Empire, and during the Assyrian ascendancy (seventh century B.C.), did art achieve a degree of naturalism, dynamism, and picturesqueness. Yet, in epic reliefs, in landscapes, and in architectural backgrounds, little attempt was made at perspective. On the other hand, there was a mastery in representing lions, horses, and dogs which has never been surpassed.

The architecture consisted mainly of baked-brick edifices (the best ones dating to Nebuchadnezzar's period, 604-561 B.C.) with enamel glaze added. A clay blueprint of the city of Nippur is extant. All buildings were originally on platforms out of mud reach, and, in form, rectangular parallelopipeds. Drainpipes were added to the sides of houses, and buildings were arranged with corners pointing to compass points in order that no face be permanently sunless. From the time of the First Dynasty onward, streets were planned so that main streets ran north and south and cross streets intersected at right angles.

Sumerian-Akkadian sculpture continued to develop down to the reign of Gudea (about the third millennium B.C.), only to fall into decadence with the ascension of the First Dynasty, and to be replaced in the Kassite period by a new style. This art aimed at representing nature in diorite statues, and succeeded in indicating the form in muscles and in the fold of textiles, despite the hardness of the stone used. Attempts were often made to infuse reality in these works by incrustations of stones of other colors, or metals; eye-whites were of shell, pupils of bitumen, bracelets of gold, etc.

The Mesopotamians acquired great skill in the use of metals, especially copper. Life-sized bull's horns were composed of copper leaf wrapped around a wooden core and fastened by small nails. Figurines were often accompanied by copper tablets. Engraving was highly developed, on shells in the early days, and later on cylinder seals on which kings and gods were popularly depicted, pottery and metals. Enameled brick, too, was popular both as a color decoration and for inlaying statues. The costumes of the people consisted of turbans, simple tunics or flounced skirts, fillets, wigs, jewels, and in the Akkadian age, sandals. Furniture consisted in the main of beds, various chairs, and household utensils.

One of the best ways to explore the culture of Mesopotamia is through its epic and other literary monuments. During the period of Sumerian dominance (from the beginning of the fourth to the end of the third millennium B.C.), there were developed the following:

1) Cuneiform writing, adopted by nearly all the peoples of the Near East. Without this ability to write, the cultural progress of western Asia would have been impossible.

2) Religious and spiritual concepts, together with a well-integrated pantheon, which influenced all of the peoples of the Near East including the Hebrews and the Greeks, and which permeated modern civilization by way of Judaism, Christianity, and Mohammedanism.

3) A vast and highly evolved literature, largely poetic, consisting of epics and myths, hymns and lamentations, proverbs and words of wisdom. In the cuneiform script dating back to 2000 B.C., there are clay tablets numbering over three thousand pieces which have been excavated in mounds, over two-thirds of

which were excavated by the University of Pennsylvania. These rank among the finest creations known to civilized man, the significance of which cannot be overestimated. The form and content of Hebrew and Greek literatures were profoundly influenced by these.

We learn through these archaeological discoveries many a significant idea or concept that prevailed among the people of that time. We know that illiteracy was quite uncommon, and that male and female scribes were accorded the highest dignity in their society. Schools existed where lessons were given in reading and tracing on clay the elements of cuneiform script. Models from Hammurabi's period illustrate the methods of instruction: reading and writing simple phonetic signs, grammar presented in paradigms, memory aids, elements of mathematics, weights and measures, and money values. Grammars and dictionaries were discovered in the Nippur library. Scribes held equal status with temple administrators and are mentioned even on cylinder seals. Clay envelopes were used to enclose tablets of letters, and double copies were made on envelopes and inner sealed documents to prevent falsification and to insure protection. Letters during the Akkadian period were strung together much like olives, laid in baskets, and tagged in metal or clay to the sender—very similar to our way of packaging things today.

The preserved literature consists of transcribed laws, copied legends, ritual formulae, prayers, incantations, and epistolary correspondence, such as the letters of Hammurabi, documents concerning invasions and wars, and, in the Tel-el-Amarna letters, policies of Egypt and Mesopotamia concerning Canaan. Documentary lists of fish, fowl, and domestic animals paved the way for zoology, botany, and mineralogy. The Mesopotamians have given us many words: i.e., chicory, cassia, cumin, crocus, hyssop, myrrh, nard, and saffron.

The ritualistic and legendary literature of Mesopotamia consists of such masterpieces as the "Poem of Creation" (quoted at the beginning of this section) which exalts the god Marduk, the poems of "Gilgamesh" and the "Myth of Etana." Kramer, in his *Sumerian Literature* survey, classifies the oldest pieces of Sumerian literature in the following way: of the 1075 pieces dating from the early post-Sumerian period, 175 are epics and myths, 300 are hymns, 50 are lamentations, and 150 are proverbs and wisdom texts. A brief summary of some of the most famous of each category follows.

A. Epics:
　　1) "Enmerkar"—the exploits of a Sumerian hero in subjugating the city of Aratta.
　　2) "Lugalbanda and Enmerkar"—Lugalbanda befriends the Zu-bird, who advises him to inform his sister Inanna of the dire straits of the city of Erech.
　　3) "Lugalbanda and Mount Hurrun"—the adventures of Lugalbanda and his companions on the mountain.
　　4) "Gilgamesh and Agga of Kish"—Gilgamesh, a king-deity, is forced to acknowledge Agga as king of Erech when besieged by him.
　　5) "Gilgamesh and Huwawa"—Gilgamesh sets out for the mountain of immortality, is helped by the god Uttu who built the mountain, is warned by En-

kidu not to proceed because of the monster (Huwa-wa), attacks the monster, but is stopped by his tears and pleas, and finally brings Huwawa before the gods Enlil and Ninlil.

6) "Gilgamesh, Enkidu and the Nether World"—the Gilgamesh epic and the Huluppu-tree.

7) "Feats and Exploits of Ninurta"—

    a) Ninurta destroys the monster Kur.

    b) Builds the city of Hursag and appoints Queen Ninmah (hence, the name Ninhursag).

    c) Blesses and curses the stones.

    d) Is praised and exalted for his deeds.

8) "Return of Ninurta to Nippur"—after vanquishing the monster Kur.

9) "Inanna and Entiki"—the fight of the two.

B. Myths:

    1) "The Deluge"—the Noah story, unpublished fragments available.

    2) "Enki and Ninhursag"—epic of Paradise.

        a) Enki supplies holy Dilmun with water.

        b) Begets Uttu (female deity of vegetation).

        c) Is cursed by Ninhursag for decreeing the fate of plants.

        d) Is healed by Ninhursag, who finally creates healing deities.

    3) "Enlil and Ninlil"—explanation of the birth of the moon-god Nanna and three chthonic deities, Nergal, Ninuzu, and another.

    4) "Emesh and Enten"—agricultural myth. Emesh and Enten are demigods created by Enlil. Enten is a field worker, but Emesh disputes his title until Enlil's intervention. In the course of Enten's argu-

ments with Emesh, he interpolates a prayer for the welfare of Ibi-Sin, the last of the kings of Ur.

5) "Lahar and Ashnan"—the creation of two cultural beings in charge of grain and cattle, and their descent to earth.

6) "Enki and Ninmah"—the creation of man.

7) "Enki and Sumer"—the civilizing of Sumer by Enki who appoints numerous deities to their sundry duties.

8) "Enki and Eridu"—the building of Enki's temple at Eridu.

9) "Creation of the Pickax"—creation of the *al* by Enlil and the dedication of this instrument by the gods.

10) "The Pickax and the Plow"—a charming fable in which each implement extols its own particular virtues.

11) "Inanna's Descent to the Nether World."

12) "Inanna and Enki"—concerning the transfer of civilization from Eridu to Erech. In brief, Inanna goes to Alzar to obtain decrees to remove the city of Erech and all sacred objects. Enki arranges a feast for her, but while drunk, gives her all the divine decrees. Upon recovering, he seeks to prevent her boat from reaching Erech. Several times she is brought back, but is always saved by Anu's faithful messenger, until she finally arrives safely and is extolled by the people of the city.

13) "Journey of Sin to Nippur"—Sin journeys to Nippur with gifts for father Enlil and is granted essentials for the welfare and prosperity of Ur.

14) "The Marriage of Martu."

Two of these may well serve to point out several interesting features of this type of literature and its possible bearing on the music of the period.

I. "Inanna's Descent to the Nether World." The story, in brief, concerns Inanna, Queen of Heaven, Goddess of Light, Love, and Life, who wishes to visit the nether world and free her lover Tammuz. She collects the proper decrees, adorns herself, and begins her journey, leaving instructions with the faithful messenger Ninshubur, if she fails to return within three days, to set up a hue and cry at the Divine Assembly and plead for help before the Moon-Goddess, the Wisdom-God, and others, whereupon she sets out for the nether world which is ruled by her sister, the Goddess of Darkness, Gloom, and Death. The gatekeeper questions her, but she concocts a false excuse to pass through. As she passes through the seven gates, each one tears off a part of her attire, until she arrives stark naked before her sister and the seven dreaded judges, who fasten upon her the "look of death," whereupon she is impaled on a stake. On the fourth day, the loyal servant proceeds to make the rounds of the gods to save his mistress. Finally, one of the gods creates two sexless creatures who are to sprinkle sixty times the "food of life" and the "water of life" over Inanna. This being done, she ascends from the nether world with a variety of ghosts, harpies, etc. The myth remains incomplete.

The characteristics of this work may give us a clue to the type of music which probably accompanied it. None of these works is narrative in a prose style; all have set *rhythms* and *patterns* that mark them as musical works although they lack a fixed musical notation to accompany them. "Inanna's Descent" has two chief characteristics which accent its rhythmic form:

1) Parallelism similar to works of the Bible.

> Lines 14-16:[6a] "The seven decrees she fastened at her side, she sought out the decrees, placed them at her hand, all the decrees she set up at her waiting foot . . . "

> Lines 43-47: "O Father Enlil, let not thy daughter be put to death in the nether world,
> Let not thy good metal be ground up into dust of the nether world,
> Let not thy good lapis lazuli be broken up into the stone of the stone-worker,
> Let not thy box-wood be cut up into the wood of the wood-worker,
> Let not the maid Inanna be put to death in the nether world . . . "

2) End of a phrase that is repetitious:

> Lines 126-160: Each section ends with—
> "What, pray, is this?
> Extraordinarily, O Inanna, have the decrees of the nether world been perfected,

---

6a Kramer, *Sumerian Literature, Preliminary Survey of the World's Oldest Literature.*

O Inanna, do not question the rites of the nether
world ... "
and Lines 215-218, each of which ends with—
"I am troubled."

II. "Gilgamesh" Epic.[7] In summary, Gilgamesh is
a hero, two-thirds divine and one-third mortal, who
is idolized by the people of Uruk, but whose desires
and arrogance are so strong that the people pray for
a counterpart to be created to divert Gilgamesh's
attention. This being of titanic strength, called Enkidu, is enticed to the palace, fights Gilgamesh, after
which they become inseparable friends. Desiring to
win everlasting fame for themselves, they set out on a
dangerous expedition against an ogre called Huwawa
and kill him. Meanwhile, seeing Gilgamesh's strength
and virility, the goddess Ishtar desires to annex his
affections, but Gilgamesh, knowing her past infidel-
ities, refuses. Enraged, she sends down the "bull of
heaven" to destroy her foe, only to have Gilgamesh
and Enkidu slay it. However, the gods decide that
Enkidu must die for slaying the sacred bull. Enkidu's
death has a powerful effect upon Gilgamesh, who is
inconsolable, and after a period of deep grief, desires
to find a way of escaping the fate of mankind—death.
Setting out on a long journey to ask advice of
Utnapishtim, the Babylonian Noah, who has been

7 For four sections of the Gilgamesh epic in inlaid panels on the famous
Harp from Ur of the Chaldees, also referred to as the King's Lyre, see Plate
II, depicting (1) Gilgamesh with two bulls, (2) lion and tiger making of-
ferings, (3) a donkey playing a bull-headed lyre while a bear dances and
another smaller animal (donkey) sits with sistrum and square tambourine
in hand, and (4) the King (or god) dancing while a horned animal (calf?)
offers two cups of wine.

granted eternal life, Gilgamesh encounters many difficulties, but succeeds at last in finding Utnapishtim. The advice of this immortal is that if a man succeeds in conquering sleep, he may also conquer its twin brother, death. Very weary, Gilgamesh is unable to resist and falls asleep. As a parting gift and final trial, Utnapishtim gives Gilgamesh a sacred fruit which he must guard until he arrives home, after which he may gain immortality. On the road, Gilgamesh decides to take a swim, during which time a serpent approaches the fruit and eats it. His last hope gone, the hero decides to make the best of life and returns to his native city.

We find the same characteristics in the "Gilgamesh" epic as in the former work discussed. The very opening passage sums up the deeds of the hero and ends with a parallelism:

Lines 1-12:[8]
"He who saw everything, of him learn, O my land,
He who knew all the lands, him will I praise.
He saw secret things and obtained knowledge of
    hidden things,
He brought tidings of the days before the floods,
He went on a long journey, became weary and worn,
He engraved on a table of stone all the travail.
He built the wall of Uruk, the enclosure,
Of holy Eanna, the sacred storehouse.
Behold its outer wall, whose brightness
    is like that of copper!
Yea, look upon its inner wall, which none can equal!"

---

8 Heidel, *Gilgamesh Epic and Old Testament Parallels.*

All of epic poetry was extremely rhythmic, and like all of the art of the Babylonian-Sumerian culture, strictly symmetrical. We may presume that music tried to imitate the forms of early poetry. Instrumental music of ancient peoples held a subordinate place; therefore, some think that the repetitious phrase-endings may have been used to sum up the general mood of the verse or to fill in a song pattern while the instruments were ending the modal line.

Unfortunately, we have no real way of knowing what the music sounded like. A document dates back to about 800 B.C. concerning which Dr. Sachs, in his article on the "Mystery of Babylonian Notation,"[9] discusses the fact that this might possibly be musical notation. The small five-inch clay plaque was written by a priest of Assur on the Tigris and contains three columns of notation: in the center column the mystic legend of creation is written in Babylonian, on the right, the Semitic and Akkadian translations of it, ending with the words, "secret; for the initiated only," and in the left column, are these strange words, having no apparent meaning:

"me, me, kur, kur,

a, a, a, a,

ku, ku, lu, lu

más, más, más ..."

Meissner and Ebeling suggest that this might be musical notation and even have ventured to work out a harp notation, such as: me = pentatonic note; kur = ligatures two notes; etc.[10]

---

9 *Musical Quarterly*, XXVIII, 1941, pp. 62-69.
10 See Appendix A for a possible harp and vocal notation of a Sumerian hymn worked out by Galpin. Sachs disagrees with this and calls it "fanciful" but it presents an interesting possibility in a still unknown field.

We know considerably more about the instruments used, the place of music in the life of the people,[11] and the other arts. The magicians intoned the sacred lamentations with percussive accompaniment. The use of the big drum, *balaggu*, is depicted on a vase in the Louvre (Figure C).[12]

FIGURE C. SUMERIAN DRUM (BALAGGU)

Also a copper kettledrum is shown covered with oxhide. On the great Stele of Ur-Nammu (at the University of Pennsylvania Museum) is a drum as large as a man, with rings thickly studded with knobs.

Most of the musical instruments excavated were found in the Royal Cemetery at Ur. Philology is sometimes of help in determining what instruments were made of, i.e., *kuš* or *šur* = skin; *gi* = cane; *giš* = wood; *urudu* = metal. The common Sumerian name, for example, for the drum was *ub*, not far removed from the Akkadian *appu*. (Note:

---

11 In Galpin's *Music of the Sumerians*, he translates a clay cylinder of the Gudea period, *circa* 2400 B.C., to reveal a poem on music's purpose:

> *To fill with joy the Temple court*
> *And chase the City's gloom away,*
> *The heart to still, the passions calm,*
> *Of weeping eyes the tears to stay.*

12 The Sumerian sign for drum
   is strangely reminiscent of the Chinese hour-glass-shaped drum.

in Egyptian, *šr* plus *tbn* = frame drum; while *ma* applies to all woodwinds.) Idiophonic instruments include concussive clubs, clappers, *sistra* with horizontal bars, bells, cymbals, and rattles. (Note in Plate III a dancer using concussion sticks. The original sticks were excavated at Fara and belong to a pre-Sargonic period, probably 2500 B.C.) An inlaid mosaic discovered at Kish close to ancient Babylon demonstrates the method of use. Also mentioned are four common types of Mesopotamian drums: a shallow frame drum, six feet wide and struck simultaneously by two men at each side (Figure C); a small cylindrical drum held in a horizontal position; a large footed drum; and a small drum with one head carried vertically on the belt and struck with both hands.

Flutes were introduced into ritual use about 2600 B.C., and are mentioned on the cylinder seals of Gudea, who instructs his director of music at the Lagash Temple "to cultivate diligently flute-playing and fill the forecourt of Eninnu with joy." The vertical flute was called *ti-gi* or *ti-gu*, and was slightly longer than the *nâ* or reed-mouthpiece flute (the latter considered a plaintive instrument, and characteristically used for laments). Galpin mentions that in an experiment exact reproductions of these were made, and by the aid of a small beating reed used in the Syrian *zumârah*, the following scale was derived:

FUNDAMENTAL   HARMONICS

Also, double silver and reed pipes with three and four fingerholes, approximating the whole-tone scale and dating back to 2800 B.C., were discovered at the cemetery at Ur, which proves that double oboes are of Semitic origin since they predated Egyptian use by 1300 years. The Hebrew flute (*halil*) is derived exactly from the Akkadian *hal-hallatu*. These wind instruments were often ornate, and richly decorated with colored stones. In a Sumerian hymn, Ishtar requests one to play for her "on the pipe (*malilu*) of lapis lazuli and pearl." For the double oboe excavated at Shem near Ur in the Royal Cemetery (*circa* 2800 B.C.), see Plates IV, V, VI, in which these pipes appear in their present broken condition as in the University Museum, in a reconstructed state (by Jesse-Phillips Robertson), and their manner of performance as shown on a terra cotta figurine from the First Babylonian Dynasty at Nippur. Note the divergent position; Curt Sachs suggests that this position is indicative of double oboes instead of double flutes or double clarinets which usually appear parallel. This is the earliest extant double oboe. As no reeds were found, it is conceivable that the cane probably disintegrated with age. A clay plaque at the University Museum also illustrates two female musicians playing a double flute and a drum on a podium in what is probably a temple scene, suggesting part of a ritual.

The trumpet, too, is mentioned in the Gudea period: *si-im* means a horn and wind. Other types would include the *gi-sal*, said, on a tablet at the Temple at Eridu, to "make a noise like a bull," implying that it may have been a gourd-type of horn with a V-shaped opening. (See Plate XXVII for a polyglobular gourd-type trumpet from Damascus, for an instrument which may be similar, though of

later origin.) The *karan*, mentioned in a letter of the King
of Mitanni to Amenophis III (*circa* 1380 B.C.), was a
similar wind instrument probably overlaid with gold.

In the grave of Lady Shubad, among inlays, lamps,
games, etc., were found numerous stringed instruments,
particularly harps and lyres. Sumerian lyres were asymmetrical, the heavier part often ornamented and held away
from the player. Lyres, called *giš-al-gar*, were graceful,
usually small of body, averaging from five to eleven strings.
Bodies symbolized royal beasts: the cow, the bull, the calf,
the donkey, or the stag. The most beautiful of these are
the head pieces of two majestic bulls. The King's Lyre,
also called the Harp of Ur, at the University of Pennsylvania Museum, has a magnificent animal with the finest
shell, lapis, limestone inlaid front below the head, showing
scenes of the Gilgamesh story, and animals with stringed
instruments and rattle. (Refer to Plates I and II.) The
British archaeologist, C. Leonard Wooley, suggests that
the fronts show the *range* of the instruments; hence, a
bull-headed lyre proves to have a bass range, a cow-headed
one a tenor range, and a calf- or stag-headed one an alto
range; i.e., an ancient three-piece orchestra. In the
"Peace Scene" of the inlaid Standard of lapis and shell, the
king sits, cup in hand, among friends, while before them a
musician plays on an eleven-stringed lyre decorated with a
bull's head, a strap over his left shoulder to support the
instrument. A woman also is depicted, hand on chest,
singing. The lyre frequently accompanied the voice. In a
hymn to Ishtar of 2100 B.C., the poet says, "I will speak
to thee with the *al-gar*, whose sound is sweet."

The harp, *giš-zag-sal*, had a plane of strings vertical

to the soundboard. Harp frames were either arched or elongated on one end or angular and held at body-neck angle. The harp of the queen was completely reassembled into a graceful boat-shaped instrument with gold knobs upon the eleven-stringed posts. The body terminated in a golden calf's head with lapis lazuli hair and beard, shell and lapis eyes, a mosaic-studded collar, a spacious wooden soundbox with inlaid edges of mosaic, red limestone, shell, and lapis.[13] Another harp showed fifteen strings, while a third only four. The inscription by the Governor of Gudea (1000 years later than this period) described a harp he had presented to a temple, decorated with a bull, the sound of which compared to the bellowing of a bull. Undoubtedly, instruments were sacred, dedicated to various gods, especially to the bull-god Nanaar. The body of the instrument usually represented the animal's body, the rear-post the tail, with legs attached to the instrument much like animal legs. These instruments were played either standing or seated, or carried in processions preceded by a small boy bearing a harp. Cylinder seals reveal uses of the harp and other instruments. One shows a woman harpist standing and playing before a queen who dines in state. The harp is crescent-shaped and has four strings. Another seal shows a king and queen at dinner with a seated musician strumming on a five-stringed harp, two cymbal players wielding instruments similar to a curved

13 See Plate VII for the silver boat-shaped lyre with the stag excavated from the Death Pit, *circa* 3000 B.C., and compare with the classical *cithara*, Plate X, from a later period. The *cithara* is constructed of two vertical posts and a horizontal crosspiece over a sounding board across which the strings are tied. The figure holds a plectrum in the right hand.

horn, while a fourth person claps hands and sings. Another seal shows only singers at a dinner-orchestra, clapping to a marked cadence.[14]

The lute, *sinnitu*, appears in Mesopotamia in the second millennium B.C., at approximately the same time as the Egyptian *nefer*. The idea for this instrument, a small soundbox and a long neck on which strings could be stopped by the fingers, must have arisen from the hunting bow or primitive musical bow.[15] This instrument became widely known throughout the Near East as the *tanbour* (compare the Sumerian *pan-tur*, the Greek *pandoura*, the Russian *balalaika*, and the Georgian *tar* from Tiflis—a notched lute with movable gut frets and parchment sound-board, shown on Plate XXIV).

Sumerian texts of the third millennium B.C. mention ecclesiastical music. In the temple of Ningirsu at Lagash, an officer was responsible for training the choir, another for training the classes of singers and players, male and female. The guild of temple singers edited and studied official liturgical literature, particularly at the college of the temple of Bel in Babylon. There were also centers of music at Shamash in Sippar, at Enlil in Nippur, at Innini in Erech. Folk music, also, had its place, as can be seen by the shepherd piping or strumming a long-necked lute to dogs and sheep on plaques and seals of the third millenium B.C. (see Plate VIII).

Music, in ancient Mesopotamia, was connected with

---

14 Two other types of harps are the Harp from Ur, Plate I, and a horizontal nine-stringed harp played while marching, Plate IX.

15 In Plate VIII a shepherd is playing a lute to his dogs. Compare this instrument with Figure A and with the Egyptian lute in Plate XI.

the planetary system, with seasonal and astronomical variations. Among most early peoples, the distribution of notes
in ancient scales was related to the distribution of planets
in the solar system. Women played their part in musical
functions; priestesses played and sang in the temples, as
did the noblewomen (the mother of Sargon and Akkad,
and the mother of Gilgamesh were priestesses who performed musical functions). The granddaughter of Naram-
Sin was a lyre-player to the god Sin. In the Kassite period,
a *kuddurru* (boundary stone) shows a woman bearing a
quiver and bow and playing a tambourine in a procession
of priest musicians. In the epoch of Gudea, a woman is
depicted beating a large drum.

The arts were inseparable from the first: where people
had singing, dancing undoubtedly accompanied it; where
they had instrumentalists, literary texts were generally
discovered. Just as drama, in later civilizations, helped to
coordinate all of the arts, so, in the earlier cultures, the
temple schools and liturgical rituals preserved for the people a unity of art.

CHAPTER II

EGYPT:

ZENITH OF HAMITO-SEMITIC CIVILIZATION

THE EARLIEST INHABITANTS OF EGYPT BELONGED TO AN exceedingly remote period of which almost no trace remains. The forefathers of the Egyptians had affinities with the Libyan tribes of North Africa, who were white-skinned and of possible European origin, and also with such African tribes as the Somalis and Gallas. In prehistoric times, the race received the addition of an element of the Semitic peoples by incursion of that group. The Egyptian language, too, had certain affinities with the Semitic tongues.

Graves have been discovered dating back to the pre-dynastic race, apparently a dark-haired people, wearing a scant minimum of clothing, and occasionally tattooing parts of their bodies. They lived in wattle and mud houses, ate food with ivory spoons, and hunted with the most skillfully wrought weapons of flint. In addition, they built vessels for trade, warfare, and pleasure voyages, and used the sail frequently. In the early tombs, we find no traces of mummification. We discover, however, numerous utensils containing food and tablets bearing incantations. Artifacts such as these reveal the Egyptian preoccupation with death and the belief in the continuation of life on a quasianthropomorphic level.

By the time of the First Dynasty (3400 B.C.), Egypt had reached a skill in design and workmanship which enabled her to make furniture and utensils of considerable beauty. The king's furniture consisted of finely carved alabaster and other stones, copper pots, ivory and ebony inlaid cabinets with legs fashioned like a bull's, exquisite gold ornaments, and statues.

In the Fourth Dynasty, the term Per-O (Pharaoh), meaning "great door," was applied to the monarch much as "Sublime Porte" was later applied to the government of Turkey. Royalty was required to be well-educated, cultured, athletic, and capable of taking any office, such as judge, at a moment's notice. The land was divided into forty sections, or *nomes*, each of which provided a militia. The capital was not fixed, but usually was situated near the Pharaoh's pyramid. Women held a high position in Egypt. Inheritance passed on through the female line, and monogamy ruled for commoners. Women were taken along for hunts, yachting trips, and fishing trips. Trade was carried on by means of barter with fixed values to gold and copper rings, the latter serving most commonly for currency. The pyramid age already knew of copper drainpipes and all complete plumbing facilities. In pottery, closed kilns were already used, fine glass objects were manufactured; fabrics were finely woven, resembling silk in texture, for weaving had reached a high level. Furniture was excellently carved of wood, overlaid with gold leaf. Wood was scarce and expensive but frequently used, nevertheless, in furniture, house fittings and shipbuilding. In the tomb of the queen mother of Khufu (Cheops), copper needles are extant. Dainty toilet spoons were carved to hold cosmetics, frequently in the form of dancers, lotuses, boating parties, musicians, flower-picking scenes, water-fowl, and some even containing inscribed love songs. Farming of this period was advanced, masonry very skilled, and the methods of smiths and miners quite modern. The high development of the jeweler's and lapidary's art is apparent when we observe diadems of the Twelfth Dynasty, among the most exquisite art of Egypt.

Pictures on the tombs of courtiers depict daily life with exquisite accuracy. On one tomb painting we note such scenes as the owner being seated in a palanquin while slaves who carry him sing hymns, the wife coming to greet him in the garden, the family reclining while playing a game of draughts and listening to the music of the harp played either by the wife or by a three-piece orchestra consisting of a harp, a pipe and a lute, or watching women entertainers in slow and stately dances. Meanwhile, the children are swimming in the pool, chasing fish, playing with a ball or doll or a jumping jack, or teasing a tame monkey under the father's ivory-legged stool.

The Middle Kingdom period (from the Twelfth Dynasty to the Hyksos invasions) produced several wonderful literary monuments. One of the greatest of these was the story of the traveler, Sinouhe (a Ulysses story), which describes vividly the living conditions in Asia and Egypt. Fragments of this romance were found in tombs, apparently included to entertain the dead. Another classic piece of this period was the "Song of the Harper," similar in theme to Ecclesiastes of the Bible. (See Appendix B.)

The establishment of the New Kingdom (1580 B.C.) restored liberty and established the capital at Thebes. Where feudalism formerly ruled, royal ownership of land took over now. Commoners could rise in civil service to the post next to the king (as in the Joseph story of the Bible). Some famous names of the period are Thothmes, Hatshepsut—the warrior-queen who wore a beard, and Amenhotep IV who radically changed the art, society, and religion of his day and introduced religious concepts close to monotheism into Egypt. Unfortunately, after his death, art and literature were restored by the priestly caste to their earlier forms. However, this great man, commonly known by his changed name, Akhnaton, left a tremendous influence on the rest of the world. One of the world's first great idealists and individualists, he may have influenced his people along the lines of monotheism and the concept of an inter-national divinity, encouraged that the stylization of art be dropped and that natural lines be emphasized instead (note informal pictures of him kissing his queen Nefretiti, and note scenes depicting him unflatteringly yet truthfully: long face, heavy thighs, etc.), and developed a new aspect of literature in the beautiful hymns to Aton.

The society of the Nineteenth and Twentieth Dynasties had changed. Feudal aristocracy had passed, and no longer were there great local princes to deal with. The marriages of brother and sister in the royal lines now became customary. Palace life grew more luxurious, simple dress was superseded by elaborate costumes and the royal harems were enormous. The two privileged classes remaining were high-ranking army officers and members of the priesthood. The armed forces consisted chiefly of archers, heavily armed infantry, and charioteers. The people were either extremely wealthy or starving poor. A rich literary output of this period dealt with exploits, hymns, and romantic tales. Maxims were preserved, as were philosophic and religious essays and love poetry. Popular stories of the day included "Tahuti" (an Ali Baba story), "Story of the Doomed Prince," and "Tale of Two Brothers" (similar to the story of Joseph and Potiphar's wife).

Of all the arts, sculpture of this period, reliefs, and colored flat work were unequaled. Composition was remarkably interesting, as may be noted in the reliefs of Seti I at Abydos, the palace at Karnak, and Amenhotep's unfinished temple at Lugsor, challengers of any art. Cretan vessels of gold, silver, inlaid with jewels, lapis and carnelian, Cyprian ivory, bronze, and copper demonstrated the marvelous talent of Egyptian metal workers, inlayers, enamelers, and carvers. The woven tapestries from the tombs of Thothmes IV and his triumphal chariot exhibited the art of masterful weavers and decorators.

Egyptian art was essentially static. Pyramids and obelisks, as well as other abstract designs, demonstrate the impersonal and unemotional striving for permanence and absolute values. The Egyptians were keen observers of nature; they achieved perfect human proportions as early as the Fourth Dynasty and created exact, unforgettable renditions of birds and animals (particularly the dog at Beni Hasan). Man was depicted at his labors: as a hunter, warrior, dancer, servant, workman—in all phases of life. Domestic scenes were prevalent on wall paintings due to the belief that in depicting these, a comfortable existence would be secured in the after-life. Painting was basically representational. Painters rarely attempted actual perspective, three dimensions, or foreshortening. No shadows were shown, because shadows are a result of light and therefore not a permanent quality of man. Thus, in religious art the image evoked by a painting was always more important than the optical impression. Chief figures were made on a grand scale with the lesser ones smaller in size, while multitudes generally were depicted by repetition of the same figure. Hieroglyphics would be used to fill in the empty spaces and to identify objects and scenes. Color in tempera, glaring and unbroken, had a conventional usage: white for linen clothes, blue for water, green for plants, black for hair, and yellow and red dots for sand and desert. This classic style lasted until about 2200 B.C., preceded by the Golden Age (Fifth Dynasty, 2700 B.C.) and followed by the Middle Kingdom era (2200-1580 B.C.) into which a pitiless naturalism was to enter, and the New Kingdom and Eighteenth Dynasty (1580-1350 B.C.) which were to express a freer spirit, liveliness, elegance, gesture, intimacy, interest in space, in the body, and in the feminine.

In sculpture, the Egyptians created no idealized statues such as the Greeks later produced. Again the idea behind the work concerned a practical purpose in providing a resting-place for the *Ka* or soul of the dead; hence the resemblance to the actual person must be strong or the *Ka* would not recognize the true place of rest. Utmost skill was concentrated on the face. For this reason the success in exact representativeness achieved by the Egyptians has never been surpassed. Statues were frequently carved in limestone or wood, and, in order to increase the life-like quality, colored, with eyes inserted (metal pupils set in rock-crystal irises surrounded by eyeballs of opaque white quartz). Portrait statues of kings, however, were done in durable stone such as diorite, or basalt, or copper.

In architecture the arch was unknown or at least unemployed. Vertical columns were regularly used, as were horizontal roofing beams. Columns represented either palm-stems with crowns of foliage, or clustered stalks of papyrus. In the former, the stem expanded into a group of leaves which formed the capital; in the latter, the stalks were bound together beneath the heads with a fillet, and the heads were clustered together into a capital on which the architrave rested.

Egyptian literature was many-sided, consisting of god legends, moral legends, historical books, autobiographies, travel and adventure stories, fairy tales, hymns, moral and philosophical works, poetry, and scientific treatises dealing with medicine, rituals, and embalming. Among ancient literature discovered, the sacred *Drama of Osiris* was the earliest known passion play. This papyrus, dating to the eighteenth or nineteenth century B.C., is the oldest illustrated book in the world. Other interesting works discovered include several scribes' school exercise books, the Pyramid texts, two famous wisdom books known as *The Proverbs of Ptah-Hotep* and those of Kagemni, and the *Book of the Dead*.

The literary achievements of the Twelfth Dynasty in particular are unusually high, consisting of wisdom compositions, travel stories, the *Instructions of Amenemhat, Praise of Learning*, and the *Hymn of Usertsen III*.

In travel literature and hero stories character becomes

a social force—good and evil is to be answered for to the gods (note Sinouhe story). The chief papyri are divided into two categories: those dealing with the sciences and those dealing with poetry. The Edwin Smith Papyrus deals with medicine and surgery particularly, and is based on fact and not myth. The human body is discussed in great detail from the head to the thorax. Brain surgery was common, if not always effective. The heart was believed to be the driving power in a system of which it is the center. Medical stitching is mentioned also, and medical classes existed in the temples.

Beside medicine there is some mention made of other sciences. Some progress apparently had been made in astronomy; the heavens had been roughly mapped and the more prominent fixed stars identified. Arithmetic was based on the decimal system, while plane geometry rules were commonly taught in schools in computing the area of a triangle, trapezium, and circle. The mathematics employed for architectural purposes must have been extremely accurate, for the Great Pyramid, oriented with remarkable accuracy and its levels astonishingly true, has remained throughout the ages one of the great wonders of mankind.

The most famous collection of poetry is known as the "Harris Papyrus" or "Harris 500" dating back to the thirteenth century B.C. and consisting chiefly of love songs. The strophe lines are short while the construction is simple, and the words probably owed their effect to the skill of the singer or harp accompanist. The most famous of these is the "Song of the Harper."[16]

The poetry of Egypt resembles the rhythmical com-

---

16 See Appendix B for examples of Egyptian poetry and other literary forms.

positions of the Hebrews in the use of parallelism, allitera-
tion, and metaphors. Three types of poetry of the two
groups can be compared:

TYPES	EGYPTIAN	HEBREW
1) Religious:	Praise to Amon-Ra	Psalms
2) Wisdom Writings:	Teachings of Ptah-Hotep	Proverbs
3) Non-religious or Lyrical:	Love Poems	Song of Songs

Gaston Maspero[17] describes the funeral of the priest
Nefu-ho-tep in the following way.

"The harpist chanted 'Be happy then, O priests! ...
Songs and music are before thee, cast behind thee all care.'
After the tomb has been sealed the family returns to a
funerary feast at which the second harpist plays a prelude,
standing before the statue of the deceased, chanting the
dirge: 'The world is but perpetual movement and change.
Not all the lamentations in the world will restore happiness
to the man who is in the sepulchre; make then a good day
and do not be idle in enjoying. Let thy face be bright
what time thou thyself livest;—Has anyone ever come out
of the coffin after once having entered it?' Dancers and
singers were hired to attend the 'Feast of Eternity' held
in honor of the dead. Music of harps accompanied the
body, along with tiny effigies of harpists and drummers."

---

17 Maspero, *Dawn of Civilization in Egypt and Chaldea.*

Dancers and musicians assisted in particular religious rites and in all festivals. Wealthy Egyptians retained a household orchestra, indispensable for their luxurious feasts and for all forms of entertainment, for music was considered an important moral and educational guide. Plato declared that Egyptian moral standards were far superior to those in his own country and that certain types of music were considered either morally elevating or degrading.

Music, as a science as well as an art, came under the guidance of priests. State laws which held national art and architecture under complete control, bound music, too, forbidding deviation from the 3000-year-old system. Certain songs were taught by law to children, while others were strictly guarded from their hearing. Interesting to note, musical traits, contrary to present views, were presumed to be of a hereditary nature, and musicianship as a profession was acquired only by inheritance. Fine schools existed, notably at Memphis, which specialized in the training of musicians. Singing was often unaccompanied in musical performances by women, while men, on the other hand, sang with accompaniment. Quite frequently, singers clapped to the rhythm of the dance accompaniment. Songs were frequently of great beauty. One of the most rhythmic work-day songs, and the oldest Egyptian song known, is the "Oxen Song":

> *Thresh for yourselves, Oxen!*
> *Thresh for yourselves!*
> *Straw for your fodder,*
> *Corn for your masters;*
> *Give yourselves no peace!*

Singers and instrumentalists were of the priestly class; in fact, instruments often were dedicated to the worship of particular gods: bells and flutes related to Osiris, the sistrum to Isis, the lyre to Thoth, the harp to Ptalu (the fire god), while Hathôr was the patroness of music and the dance. Orchestras are described of as many as six hundred players on harps, lyres, sistra, tambouras, and flutes. Mention is made of the Ptolemies who employed choruses of hundreds of voices, accompanied by hundreds of harps and flutes. The temples were so spacious that, undoubtedly, a great volume of sound was necessary in order to hear clearly.

Theaters were unknown, but much private entertainment and large ceremonials made up for the loss. Originally the earliest gestures of formal performance consisted of quiet pacing, later becoming more vivid with ceremonial flashing cymbals, tambourines, castanets, and more acrobatic with pirouetting, extreme posturing, juggling, leaping, and sensuously graceful somersaulting. Acrobats as well as dancers were attached to the temple service; both men and women trained for these jobs, and hired as private entertainers, accompanied by monkeys. Song and dance were generally accompanied by the clapping of hands. The blind harpist also was a familiar figure in Egypt, always present at private entertainment, or represented on a wall painting as playing before the king. A group of figurines from an excavated grave of about 1400 B.C. shows a noble lord seated before his cabin in a royal barge, breathing the fragrance of lotus buds and listening to the music rendered by a blind harpist, who is seated upon a small stone and holding his seven-stringed harp between his knees, while a singer stands nearby hand over mouth to form a tremolo, commonly used in singing. Another grave yielded a mechanical toy which was made up of a group of musical dancing dolls.

Nearly 1300 years after this came the barge that bore Cleopatra upon her visit to Mark Antony. Plutarch describes it thus: "Her barge in the river of Cydmus, the poop whereof was gold, the sails of purple, and the oars of silver, keeping stroke in rowing, often the sound of the music of the flutes, oboes, harps, viols (no doubt, tambouras), and such other instruments as they played upon the barge." Plutarch tells us, moreover, that Cleopatra entertained her noble guests with music. Female musicians, with harps, lutes, and lyres, played for them, and other musicians came from Syria with lovely dancing girls. Her father Ptolemyauletes was so named to indicate his love for music (auletes meaning "flute-lover"). Other Ptolemies, too, were known for lavish musical displays.

The golden period of Egyptian music lasted from 2500 B.C. until the land was invaded by the Persians and the Greeks. Indicative of the close relationship between music and dancing are the paintings of singers and dancers depicted with instrumentalists.[18] Capart,[19] in speaking of the early art of Egypt, discusses primitive dance, which was, at first, of a magical-utilitarian nature, its chief purpose being to strengthen men in battle and to aid the gods in

---

18 Plate XI depicts an all-girl chamber orchestra of the Eighteenth Dynasty performing on a curved harp, lute, double oboe and oblique lyre with plectrum. A small apprentice in the center accompanies them or possibly sings along. It is suggested that the three center musicians are more scantily attired than the end ones because they also served in the capacity of dancers.
19 Capart, *Primitive Art in Egypt.*

the fructification of the earth (fetish men were both dancers and skilled musicians). Later the dance developed a
pleasurable, more entertaining purpose. Throughout primitive times, however, music remained merely an accompaniment to dancing or singing.

In the days of the Old Empire, Egyptian dance was
slow and simple with rhythmic accompaniment by four
female singers.[20] There were usually from three to twelve
dancers, men and women, who danced on such occasions
as the "Feast of Eternity" (to the dead), the harvest festival of the first fruits to "Min," and for the pleasure of
the goddesses Hathôr and Bastet.

In the Eighteenth Dynasty steps became rounded and
gliding, the attitudes less angular than those of the Old
Kingdom. Musical performance passed partly into the
hands of women (usually foreign girl musicians), and became more sensual, while a more refined tonal system came
into vogue, based on the division of the string plus cycles
of fifths and fourths.[21] The dance, meanwhile, had grown
more coquettish in the New Empire,[22] accompanied by
tambourines or castanets and a single flute. Each large
household had a "superintendent of the singing," who
acted also in the capacity of the superintendent of the
harem. The royal harem was particularly adept at enter-

---

20 Erman, *Life in Ancient Egypt.*
21 More concerning the tuning of instruments under a later section on instruments.
22 An interesting group of musicians playing double oboe and clappers, and
rather spirited dancers are depicted on Plate XII, from a painting in the
tomb of Tuthmosis IV or Amenophis III. The double-oboe player is
painted in the rare full-faced position, possibly because she was not considered a "lady." Note ornaments and careful shading of the feet, exem-
plary of the freer spirit of art.

taining, and would "daily rejoice the heart of the king with beautiful songs and fulfill every wish of the king by their beautiful singing."

Priests always sang to harp or flute accompaniment while women generally sang *a cappella*. Men, however, were regarded as artists, while women were considered to be mere accompanists in their singing. Both kept time by clapping, which was inseparable from correct singing—in fact, the verb "to sing" was represented by the sign of the hand.

Egyptian paintings depict singers who bring the left hand to the left ear in the typical Oriental gesture. (A wall plaque from a Theban tomb portrays singers with one hand held partly out with thumb and forefinger forming a circle and other fingers held stiffly, while the other hand is placed on the ear or on the knee in a relaxed position.) Wrinkles carefully drawn between the eyebrows indicate nasal singing from a compressed throat at a high pitch. The right arm is used for gesturing to the accompanist—palm upward, thumb up, or thumb bent against forefinger, or palm downward.[23] Audible time-beating was common in Egypt. The tomb of Amenemhêt, at Thebes (after 1500 B.C.), depicts a conductor standing before and facing performers, and pounding time with the right heel while snapping thumbs and forefingers.

Research in musical instruments of Egypt is facilitated by (1) the extremely arid soil, which preserved hundreds of instruments from decomposition, and (2) belief in the magic power of painting and sculpture, which left reproductions of domestic and other phases of life on the

---

23 It is interesting to note that Hindu singers beat time with the same gestures.

walls to aid in the next life. Even the names of the instruments are frequently marked on the paintings. In the eighteenth century B.C., when Egypt conquered southwestern Asia, subjugated kings sent tributes of strange new instruments and musicians. In one painting in the Amarna residence of Amenophis IV, singing and dancing girls are shown practicing in the harem. Nearly all ancient instruments were at this time discarded: the standing harp became larger with added strings, while new types of harps were introduced; oboes replaced flutes; and lyres, lutes, and drums became popular. Music had become much noisier. Curiously, many instruments of the West had been placed simultaneously in Egypt, Palestine, Phoenicia, Syria, Babylonia, Asia Minor, Italy, and Greece, the latter using exclusively Semitic names for their instruments. Hand-beaten drums, double oboes, which permitted drone techniques, and fretted lutes exemplify the oldest type of autonomous instrumental melody and refined rhythm. In this area, cosmopolitan reciprocity prevailed, for during 3000 to 4000 years of ancient history, these countries formed a musical province in which free intercourse created understanding in musical exchange. Even under Islam, and with the loss of Greece, this area remained united, due to the fact that the Mohammedans built their music upon the fundamentals of Greek theory.

TYPES OF INSTRUMENTS

I) PERCUSSIVE:

    a) Concussion sticks—used in early fertility rites.[24]

    b) Clappers—made of metal, bone, or ivory, sometimes shaped like boomerangs, some resembling gazel-

---

24 Similar to the Mesopotamian percussion sticks of the pre-Sargonic era, Plate III.

le-heads, and extended in unison by a group of posturing dancers. A pair of ivory clappers shaped
like human hands, dating back to the Eighteenth
Dynasty, are in the Metropolitan Museum in New
York. The clappers are actually the most primitive
musical instrument known to Egypt, and used exclusively to accompany dances. While many are
shaped like boomerangs, it is believed that their
primary extra-musical purpose was to frighten away
or kill birds. A prehistoric dance at El Amreh (*circa*
3400 B.C.) shows a woman dancing while two men
accompany her with clappers.

c) *Sistra*—called *seshesh* or *kemkem*—connected with
the Isis cult. Figure D is a *naos sistrum* or temple

FIGURE D. NAOS SISTRUM   FIGURE E. BULLROARER

sistrum with Hathôr's head. The typical *sistrum* consisted of a bronze or copper handle in a narrow, inverted horseshoe-shape with crossbars inserted loosely
horizontally across the middle. It was used by priestesses to drive away evil spirits. Drawings in the tomb

of Rameses II show his queen holding two *sistra*. Another type of *sistrum* is the bull-roarer (Figure E), consisting of a flat, usually rectangular board, revolving upon a handle at right angles and producing a roaring or whistling vibration. The *menyet* was a later addition to the *sistrum* family. A bronze counterpoise strung with beryl, bronze, and faïence beads was discovered dating back to the Twenty-sixth Dynasty, *circa* 600 B.C. (Now in the Metropolitan Museum.)

d) Castanets—called *crotala*, made of metal with knobs. Used in pairs, they were struck together while dancing.

e) Cymbals—of silver or brass, frequently were dainty, scallop-edged, and worn on fingers like the sagget type. Cymbals were a favorite, and frequently buried with mummies. The sacred musician Ankhape was buried with his cymbals. Cymbals, together with the *sistrum* and *menyet*, formed the chief instrumental ensemble for religious occasions.

f) Bells—mainly used in religious ceremonies, such as at the feast of Osiris, or to summon worshipers. According to Hickmann,[25] early Egyptian camel-bells may have had quite an extensive range of sound—

<hr />

25 Hans Hickmann, *Zur Geschichte der Altägyptischen Glocken.*

g) Tambourines—round or rectangular, with incurving side and a narrow frame with crossbars in the middle, were used chiefly to accompany dances. In his article on the rectangular tambourine, Hickmann [26]suggests a rhythmic beat for the performer:

Right Hand

Left Hand

h) Drums—three types common:
   1) elongated barrel-shape with parchment head which swung from the neck of the performer by a leather strap and was played with the hands. This and the cylinder drum were the earliest types used.
   2) short, wide, circular type, also swung from the neck and played with curved drumsticks.
   3) smaller type carried beneath arm or hand, narrow neck used as handle and played with fingers or knuckles of the right hand.

Drums did not appear in Egypt until 2000 B.C In later ages there were drums galore, in cup and vase shapes of gourd or parchment, skin or metal. The modern Egyptian *darabukkah* is descended from the spherical-shaped drum or tambourine.

II) WIND:
   a) Flutes—*sebi*, single, vertical flute held obliquely,

---

26 Hans Hickman, "*Le Tambourin Rectangulaire du Nouvel Empire*," from *Miscellanea Musicologica*.

dates back at least to 3000 B.C. Originally of bone, this was later made of cane, a yard long, half inch bore, containing two to six fingerholes with a possible thumbhole. Great versatility in tone was achieved by changing the angle of playing. Long flutes (Figure F), like those later adopted by the Persians, were held

FIGURE F. EGYPTIAN MUSICIANS PLAYING
LONG FLUTE AND TRUMPET

at a sloping angle and stopped by the fingers, while shorter ones were played vertically. The transverse flute was used in the worship of Serophis. However, in the New Empire, these types were superseded by double flutes or pipes, called *mam*, played chiefly by women for the dance. Usually one pipe carried the melody, the other accompanying it. The two double flutes found in the tomb of Lady Maket, which are 3000 years old, are twenty-four inches long, very slender, of thin cane or hollow water-reed, and blown across like whistles. The holes, three on one, four on the other, are graduated in size, oval, and orange-stained and waxed.[27] The flute was probably indigenous to Egypt. In the Ashmolean Museum at Oxford, a prehistoric slate palette, dating back approximately to 3200 B.C., pictures a number of animals, among whom stands a hunter disguised as a jackal, enticing his prey with the sweet strains of the flute. This is the earliest representation of this musical instrument in Egypt.

b) Clarinets and oboes—double clarinets are depicted on reliefs from 2700 B.C., made of twin parallel cylinders of cane with properly angled reed mouthpiece, usually with a few fingerholes. Two holes were often stopped with one finger across them. In the New Kingdom, the oboe was a double reed instrument, about two feet long and a half inch in diameter. The longer one served as a drone accompaniment, its holes being stopped with wax. Curt Sachs classifies pairs of pipes in a divergent position as being double oboes, while those held in a parallel position are supposedly double clarinets.[28]

c) Trumpets—a variety of trumpets existed. Some, three feet long, of copper or bronze, were used in battle (c. 1415 B.C.) Of yellow metal, conical-shaped, with mouthpiece and a wide bell, others were two

---

27 Referred to by Smith in *The World's Earliest Music*, and in the *Musical Times*, Oct. 1, 1890, "Recent Discovery of Egyptian Flutes and Their Significance." In speaking further on double flutes, Manusues says in an article in the same periodical, Dec. 1, 1890, on "Egyptian Flutes," that in the Egyptian theater the higher flute, generally carrying the melody, was held toward the audience, while the lower one faced the actors.

28 See Plates XI and XII for double oboes. For a more modern example of the twin clarinet, see Plate XIII, a Moroccan *zummâra settauia*. This cane instrument was probably derived from ancient Egypt. The twin cane clarinets have six frontal stops each.

feet long, and used for the worship of Osiris. A range of a twelfth on this type is probable. Two trumpets were found in the tomb of Tutankhamon, one of silver, the other of copper, both overlaid with gold. The silver trumpet measured twenty-two and one-half inches, while the copper one was only nineteen and one-half inches in length. Both ended with flares or "bells." The twin trumpets are thought by some to be of Israelitish origin and brought to Egypt at a later date. An Eighteenth Dynasty tomb painting at Thebes depicts a model military band composed of trumpets, drum, and clappers. (See Figure F).

III) STRINGS:

a) Harps—numerous types of harps were popular. The most magnificent of all harps was the standing harp of Rameses III (*circa* 1230 B.C.), seven feet tall, and decorated with paintings and mosaics. One standing harp with fourteen strings dates from 1425 B.C. The very earliest harps were curved in a crescent shape like a hunter's bow, many dating before 1500 B.C. (we hear of the harp from 3000 B.C.). Some bow-shaped harps were carried on the shoulder, while others were held upright. In the Metropolitan Museum, a paddle-shaped knee-harp of the Twelfth Dynasty is exhibited, on which four strong pegs are still extant. Size varied from arm size to harps seven feet tall. The *buni*, twenty-one-stringed with ornate designs, was a favorite. The catgut strings numbered from five to twenty-two, generally, though in the New Empire, two kinds achieved top popularity: one with six or seven strings and a larger one with twenty strings. Pegs at the top were for adjustment, but no pillar insured accurate tuning.[29] Strings were always plucked with the fingers or a plectrum, never with hammers like the Arabian *santu*. In the New Kingdom, a small shoulder-harp, as well as a *trigonon*, a small three-stringed harp, appeared. At funerals, it was customary for the harpist to kneel while playing a larger harp. The triangular harp achieved great popularity, elaborately painted and decorated, tasseled and padded, some even with leopard skins and other luxurious materials draped over them.[30]

Four basic types of harps included (1) the arched harp which stood on the ground with vertical strings facing outward and the body next to the player, and was usually played by a kneeling man (see Figure G, II); (2) the footed harp which rested on a slanting leg (see Figure G, I and IV); (3) the shoulder-

I II III IV

FIGURE G. EGYPTIAN STRINGED INSTRUMENTS

---

29 Frontal pillars were used predominantly in European harps. Since many Semitic harps were reinforced with metal or ivory, the frontal pillar may not have been necessary to insure tuning.

30 Note such a harp in Plate XI.

harp, borne on the left shoulder and played with hands uplifted, probably tuned in fourths, fifths, and octaves (called by Josephus "*organon trigonon en-armonion*," possibly tuned pentatonically without half tones); and (4) the angular, Asiatic harp, which had a straight, narrow body with open front, the body being sewn into a piece of leather which served partly as a soundbox, the strings facing outward and numbering twenty-one to twenty-three, fastened in position to tasseled knobs. Figure H is an example of

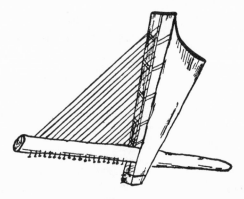

FIGURE H. ANGLE HARP

an angle harp exhibited in the Metropolitan Museum, and dates back to a late period, probably Thirtieth Dynasty (*circa* 300 B.C.). Twenty small pegs on the transverse bar indicate the number of strings, although the author counted twenty-seven holes in the upright pillar, which may refer to additional strings or to additional possible tuning positions. Decay of the wood is, of course, a further consideration.

b) Lyres—said to be the invention of the god Thoth, who, like Apollo, found music in an empty tortoise shell. Generally V-shaped, lyres had five to twenty strings fastened to a wooden horseshoe frame, and were usually held upright on a stand or supported on the player's lap. The lyre became fashionable in the Eighteenth Dynasty, so much so, that its popularity eventually superseded that of the harp; in fact, its use was jealously guarded from other countries. All shapes and sizes existed, ranging from five-stringed lyres usually played by the ladies, to eighteen-stringed six-footers which required standing performers. There were two chief types: (1) the New Kingdom lyre, shallow with a square soundbox and with two divergent asymmetrical arms and oblique crossbar, the strings being probably tuned pentatonically (Figure G, III, and Plate XI); and (2) the new Asiatic type which appeared after 1000 B.C., and consisted of a small, symmetrical rectangle with parallel arms and a crossbar at right angles.

c) Lutes—called *nefer, tamboura* or *nabla,* they were a great favorite, appearing on numerous wall paintings, sculptured panels, even on the scarabaeus, and representing in hieroglyphics the single attribute: good. Maspero says, in his *Legendary History of Egypt,* that the same articulations, *nafir* and *naufu,* convey in Egyptian the idea of a lute and the idea of beauty, the symbol expressing both at the same time. Dating earlier than 1500 B.C., and imported from Asia, lutes were in the main womanly instruments while harps were played more often by men. Shown with orchestras,[31] with solo players, with dancers playing as they danced, the popularity of the lute is obvious. Lutes,

---

31 Refer to Plate XI for this instrument.

long and slim of neck, some with frets and two to
five pegs for strings, seemed to indicate a mood of
gaiety with ribbons looped to the players' shoulders
and tassels dangling from pegs. Frequently keystone-
shaped or melon-shaped or greatly attenuated, one of
the most popular types was the *te-bouni*, a banjo-like,
three-stringed instrument with moon-shaped body
and parchment head dating 500 B.C.[32] The earliest
evidence of the use of the fingerboard can be found in
a mural painting in Nakht's tomb at Thebes showing
a lutanist playing a western Asiatic lute with nine
frets on its very long neck. Frets were first equi-
distantly placed, but since this was unsatisfactory
except for octaves, the division principle of dividing
the strings into half, quarter, etc., in order to attain
desirable tones, gained vogue.

Obviously, there were musical systems in the ancient
world, even if no records of them remain. It is believed
that the Greeks, borrowing their musical system from
Egypt, may have based their notation on that of Egypt.
No fixed harmony or notation is recorded. All systems
followed one trend—to make a bold plunge to the nearest
consonant note, the fourth, the fifth, the octave. These
give melodic range to the solid skeleton, and stress certain

---

32 That Egyptian instruments were numerous and portrayed with amazing
frequency on tomb illustrations showing how important their function was
in society, can readily be seen by their number and variety shown on the
plates of Schaefer and Andrae's *Kunst des Alten Orients*. This writer, after
careful study of these plates, has noted the following instruments: harps,
flutes, double flutes, oboes held at eye-level, *sistra* (bronze, wood, alabaster),
drums, lutes; also singers, some portrayed with hand gestures to produce
falsetto singing.

notes for rest or suspension. In a jump of a fourth, by adding one or two extra inner tones, we derive a tetra-chord; in the fifth, by adding inner tones, a pentachord—which undoubtedly represent the earliest types of scales.[33]

We can probably learn a great deal concerning the scales of Egypt in studying the musical scenes of banquets, as well as temple ceremonies, on reliefs. The ensembles, many of which were actual orchestras,[34] show careful finger positions of performers, and since the Egyptians represented all things in a true and lifelike manner, we need have no fear that lack of knowledge concerning music or carelessness causes the players' hands to be portrayed inaccurately on the instruments; quite the con-trary is true. Just as the adornment of the chief instru-ments was precisely portrayed, so, too, the manner of playing on them. Concerning the harp defined by Josephus as the "*organon trigonon enarmonion*," the approximate scale derived from observing hand positions on the strings is A F E C B. Lyres, which appeared 1200 to 1300 years after harps (in the fifteenth century B.C.), were also en-harmonic, according to Josephus, but most of Egyptian music was chiefly pentatonic, consisting of the scale E G A B D.

Pipes, primitive as well as developed, had equidistant fingerholes, which, in order to produce a musical scale, must have been corrected by the size of the hole, the

---

33 Sachs, C., *The Rise of Music in the Ancient World.* Also note discussion by Smith, *The World's Earliest Music,* in quoting Ellis, saying: "Musical scales are naturally diverse and unnatural to the primitive ear."

34 One relief shows seven harps and seven flutes. In many reliefs, artists may have reduced the number of players due to lack of space. Singers were also always included, although not much room may have been left to por-tray the precise number.

breath, the fingering, or by some special device. Of the
two Egyptian flutes discovered in a tomb of the Middle
Kingdom, (*circa* 2000 B.C.), one, 95 centimeters long, has
holes placed at 10/15, 11/15, and 13/15 of its length, while
the other, 90 centimeters long, measures holes 8/12, 9/12,
and 10/12 of its length. Of Lady Maket's flutes, the four-
holed one has a fundamental tone of F, the lowest tones
being one-line E, one-line B, two-line E, to two-line Bb;
the three-holed flute a fundamental of Db, and the tones
one-line F, one-line C, two-line E.[35] Kiesewetter's
theory is that Egypt used the Pythagorean tetrachord
commonly. Of course the question can be raised that if
Egyptian flutes of the Empire period had five to six holes,
meaning a total of seven possible tones, could this not
indicate a heptonic rather than a pentatonic scale? Indeed,
it hardly seems possible that enharmonic tuning be used
on an instrument like the flute in the same manner as it
was used on the harp. Even accounting for fractional
tones, the possibility of this type of scale still presents a
question to the theorist.

---

35 See *Musical Times,* Oct. 1, 1890, "Recent Discovery of Egyptian Flutes and
Their Significance."

CHAPTER III

PALESTINE:

CROSSROADS OF CIVILIZATION

IT IS A CURIOUS FACT THAT THE CHIEF RELIGIOUS-ETHICAL text of the three great monotheistic faiths today represents the primary historical and musical source-book for the Hebrew people. The Hebrew Bible remains an encyclopedic document of the cultural life and the psychological, ethical, and artistic expression of the ancient Hebrews. It is from this source that we derive almost all of our knowledge concerning the music and the other arts of the land of the Israelites from the days of the Patriarchs until the second Exile in 70 of the Christian Era.

Abraham, the first historic character of the Hebrews,

lived about 2000 B.C.,[36] and accepted in his wanderings, searching for sustenance of body and soul, the role which destiny was to hand over to his descendants. He became the cultured wanderer, the nomad-patriarch, tasting the varieties of culture about him and converting this cross-breeding of tastes into an art that resides on a spiritual-ethical plane. Abraham brought from his native city of Ur the culture and thought of Mesopotamia, the legends of Sumer and Akkad, the laws and codes of Babylonia, to the polished court life and luxurious art of Egypt. Bearing within himself the effects of these great but divergent civilizations, Abraham welded the best parts of each unto the still barbaric culture of Canaan. He and his descendants were to add to this conglomerate culture the concept which had a tremendous effect upon Western civilization —monotheism—the worship of one all-powerful, yet invisible God. Thus, they developed the versatility of art and the stimulus of spiritual thought that made the land of the Hebrews the crossroads of civilization.

Archaeology proves the cultural relationship of Babylonia and Egypt, and reveals the role that Palestine played from earliest times—that of mediator between nations. Archaeologists have discovered in recent years the Nuzu documents at Tel-el-Amarna, which, together with the Ugaritic texts, serve as cross-references to the Biblical period. It is almost unnecessary to furnish proof that Abraham lived in the period now commonly designated as the Amarna Age; such evidence as the name Sarai, Eliezer the chief servant being chosen the first heir to

---

36 Some authorities date Abraham *circa* 1400 B.C., although it appears that most archaeologists, on the basis of most recent discoveries, date Abraham earlier.

Abraham, Sarah being obliged to provide her husband with a concubine due to her own lack of offspring, the annunciation of the birth of Isaac, the story of Lot, the negotiations concerning Jacob's birthright—all serve to illustrate common customs of the period described in the Amarna documents.

Archaeological discoveries in recent times have uncovered a number of outstanding artifacts and architectural structures which have dispelled that notion that the Hebrews possessed no fine arts other than literature and music. For one thing, scholars have been led to believe that the Canaanites, among whom the Hebrews resided, had a fairly high culture. They used four or five systems of writing, and messages from Amarna to the Egyptian court reveal letters, business documents, and administrative lists of a high level.

Life for the Hebrews in the days of the Kings was certainly not luxurious, but comfortable. Homes possessed individual cisterns in which fresh rain water was stored all year round. Emphasis was laid, by the Mosaic law, on personal hygiene and the avoidance of practices and foods conducive to the spreading of disease. Families lived in the upper story of the home, retaining the ground floor for storage and working quarters only. Subterranean drains were employed, as time passed, to keep the interior of the towns dry. Iron tools were used predominantly. Fringed tunics and mantles, short stocking caps bound like turbans, and high boots with upturned toes à la Hittite exemplified the prevailing fashion.[37]

Among the most notable architectural remains in

---

37 William F. Albright, *The Archaeology of Palestine.*

Palestine are the furnaces and refineries at Ezion-Geber on the Red Sea, which were employed in the Solomonic period (973-933 B.C.) to smelt copper ore found in the vicinity, the stables of King Solomon found at Megiddo, housing 500 horses, of which the hitching-posts carried the mangers and supported the roof, and the 120-yard tunnel cut through rock to connect the spring outside the fortress with a 180-foot-deep shaft inside the city in order to receive water. The Shiloah tunnel is also a masterpiece of engineering, conducting water from the spring of Gihon outside Jerusalem to the inner city. Constructed during the reign of King Hezekiah (*circa* 700 B.C.—II Kings 20:20), it is over 500 feet long and was to be used in case of siege.

Art works of the Ahab period (876-853 B.C.) include numerous ivory plaques, probably influenced by Phoenicia. Inlaid gold, lapis, colored stones and glass, seals, as well as wall-coverings, furniture, and household goods of this period are the mute remains of a bygone era.[38]

The development of the Hebrews as an independent nation took place progressively from the Abraham-patriarchal period, through the Mosaic establishment of a theocracy, the Deborah-Judges transition from tribalism to nationhood, and culminated in the Davidic establishment of a royal dynasty. From patriarchal times onward, music played its role as one of the chief artistic expressions of the Israelites, particularly since some types of fine arts were forbidden by the Second Commandment.[39] As early in the

---

38 Reifenberg, A., *Ancient Hebrew Arts.*

39 Despite the injunction against three-dimensional graven images, Astarte figurines and household gods (*teraphim*, mentioned in the story of Rachel stealing these from Laban before a journey), were fairly common in patriarchal times, while the era of Kings boasted of ivory figurines along with tapestries, mosaics, and other art objects. Mention is even given the chief artist-architect of the Temple, Bezalel.

Bible as the genealogies stemming from Adam, mention is made of Jubal, "the father of all such as handle the lyre and pipe."[40] Josephus ascribes the invention of the psaltery and cithara to Jubal, too, and explains the meaning of his name as being that of a musical instrument, the "ram's horn" or "loud trumpet."

The place of music in the life of the Israelites cannot be overestimated. The Bible is rich in references to musical instruments, songs, and the place of song and dance in the life of the people. In the days of the Patriarchs and Judges, music was in that primitive stage in which emotions and free effusion shaped the patterns of melody and rhythm. Everyone sang, and all women, at least, played the lyre and the timbrel. We are informed that while crossing the Red Sea, Moses struck up a tune of glorification to God, the men joining in while the women replied antiphonally. Miriam's song, at the crossing, accompanied by "timbrel and dance," Deborah's paean of victory, the welcome of Jepthah's daughter, the welcome of Saul and David on the return from their victories by the women singing, dancing, and playing instruments, serve as illustrations of the place of music as the predominant expression of art and inspiration. Music caused ecstasy to take possession of the seers (in Saul), drove the demons from Saul, and soothed the frightened shepherd (David).

The Egyptian influence on the musical development of the Israelites was considerable. The patriarchal Israelites had such poetry and music as was proper to a pastoral

40 It is interesting to note that apparently all wisdom gods were also music gods in ancient legends; i.e., the Egyptian god Thoth, credited with having written 42 books on astronomy, acoustics, music, etc., who invented the lyre; Apollo who invented and played the cithara; and Narada, the Indian god of learning, eloquence, laws, and astronomy, who invented the harp.

people. They possessed the heart and inspiration for music, but lacked the science. In Egypt, they found and adopted new instruments on which to express more adequately their musical ideas. When the family of Jacob arrived in Egypt, they were welcomed by the Hyksos, the "Shepherd Kings,"[41] who, because of a similar cultural background, could be thought of as possessing similar tastes and habits much in common with their own. Jacob settled in a community of mixed peoples at Heliopolis (On) where his family was free to develop their latent talents without undue restraint. They had brought with them the *kinnor* and the *ugav* of Jubal (Genesis 4: 21) and some other early Syrian instruments. However, it was the mathematical practices of the Egyptians, rapidly adopted by the Israelites, that permitted the music of their souls to be expressed as a science as well as an art.

There were three outstanding reasons why this musical growth was possible. First, the Israelites remained in Egypt for a duration of time sufficient to absorb almost all of the desirable portions of Egyptian culture. The subsequent two generations of wandering alone on the Sinaitic peninsula enabled the Hebrews to refine and personalize for themselves the best of this Egyptian inheritance. Secondly, during the period of bondage in Egypt, their style of living had been basically similar to that of their Egyptian contemporaries, thus enabling a sympathetic exchange of ideas. Thirdly, life under the earlier pharaohs, prior to Rameses, had been peaceful, prosperous and uplifting. As a consequence of these three reasons, the music of Egypt and of the Israelites showed many similarities, and the latter

---

41 Some authorities claim that the Hyksos may have been early Hebrews instead of an unidentifiable nomadic group.

naturally acquired the opportunity of expressing their music on the Egyptian musical instruments. The Egyptian harp went into the musical ritual of Solomon's Temple, where the *nefer* (lute) was also popular. In fact, music as used in the private and religious life of the Egyptians was taken over by the Israelites as part of their own means of expression, and certain musical rituals, such as the use of sacred bells, can be found symbolized today in the Judeo-Christian religions, on the Torah-covers of the Jews, and in the annunciatory bell of the Roman Catholics as the host is manifested to the worshipers.

Just as the Egyptian instruments were promptly adopted by the Hebrews, as exemplified by Miriam's use of the timbrel (Exodus 15: 20), so the melodies were probably used as well. Sir John Stainer has said that "the glorious song of Moses was probably sung to some simple Egyptian popular chant." Moses himself, taught science and music by Egyptian priests,[42] has lived on in Islamic tradition as the patron of pipers. Thus we can observe that Egypt allowed the Israelites to develop their musical abilities and to learn how to manufacture good instruments.

The Israelites as mediators carried this tradition wherever they went. Just as their most ancient customs, legends, and religious myths were derived from common Oriental lore but molded and interpreted by them in a new spirit, so their temple service, poetry, and art can be traced to Oriental sources, but assumed with them a distinctive character, in giving art and history a raison d'être and attributing a divine purpose to life itself. Just as new moral values, in originating with them, caused the greatest

---

42 Philo, *Contemplative Life.*

spiritual and cultural center in the ancient world to be erected, so music received new foundations upon which, one thousand years after the period of Solomon's Temple at Jerusalem, western civilization was to base its musical style.

In all highly developed civilizations, music was carried from the stage of carefree instinct and tradition to the level of law and logic, of measure and reckoning. Ranking with the liberal arts from earliest times, music permeated science, medicine, mysticism, education, politics, philosophy, physics, and magic. In Palestine, music was first used in religious rites. Singing and playing on special instruments were described in the laws of the priests. Music was declared to be a gift of God, and prophecy was meant to be sung, for musical sound was said to reverberate in space, and the spheres were declared to have a harmony similar to music (Job 38:7—"when the morning stars sang together").

The one great legendary musician of the Hebrews and the patron of music was King David. I Chronicles 15: 16-24 dates the beginning of the history of Hebrew music from David's reign. He played the cithara and harp, and demonstrated his understanding of the medicinal-neurological value of music when he played before King Saul. In II Chronicles 7:6 the organization of the Temple's musical service, the creation and melodies of the Psalms, and the invention of musical instruments are ascribed to him, as was the founding of the earliest official body of musicians to perform in honor of the Lord's tabernacle. David maintained four thousand singers and performers, of whom 288 were said to be exceedingly skillful. When he brought the Ark to Jerusalem, he appointed Levites to provide vocal and instrumental music, and named the heads of the choirs: Heman, Asaph, and Ethan—chief of cymbals, psalteries, and harps, respectively, and Chananiah, chief of song. All manner of instruments were used, from harps, psalteries, and cymbals to cornets and timbrel. David inaugurated ritualistic dancing before the Ark, which was followed in later years by processional dancing.

Music in Palestine had developed to a high point during the reign of Solomon (*circa* 1000 B.C.). The Temple chorus was so enormous that Josephus tells us that at the dedication of the Temple, Solomon hired 200,000 singers, 200,000 trumpeters, and 40,000 *sistrum* players to perform, while 120 priests were employed to sound special trumpets. The *nevel* and *kinnor* were also used, 40,000 of them. During the famous visit of the Queen of Sheba, the King was said to have spoken "3000 proverbs and 1005 songs," at which time "harps and psalteries for singers" were employed.

The Israelites considered it a becoming thing to take delight in music and in the dance, and persons of rank considered it a necessary part of their education. Careful distinction was made between sacred and profane music at public and private festivals, at funerals and at religious services. The character of the music varied according to the mood of the occasion. The importance of musicians in Palestine and the high standards of musicianship may be observed not only by the fact that musicians were carefully numbered among other exiles returning from Babylonia, but also by the fact that Sennacherib demanded as highest tribute from Hezekiah, King of Judah, women musicians.

Antiphonal singing evolved in the Temple where the

Levites and Levite daughters performed—the first pro-
fessional musicians. About 1000 B.C., foreign instruments
appeared rather suddenly as they had appeared in Egypt
after 1500 B.C.: harps, zithers, oboes, cymbals, *sistra*. The
Talmud (Shabbat 56b) tells us that when Pharaoh's
daughter married Solomon, she brought as part of her
dowry "1000 kinds of musical instruments." The kings
and queens of subsequent times supported court musicians
of both sexes. We know that of the 42,360 persons returning from the Babylonian exile, some 7000 were servants
and 200 men and women were singers attached to wealthy
households.

The Talmud describes the rituals of daily Temple
music around the beginning of the Christian Era: among
rituals of arising, washing, gathering fagots for altar and
sacrifices, the priests and Levites recited the Ten Com-
mandments, the "Hear O Israel" credo, and two passages
from the Pentateuch. After the sacrifice, the priests blew
on two silver trumpets, one priest clashed cymbals, and
the Levites broke into song. A different Psalm was sung
each day of the week and on the Sabbath: on Sunday, 24;
Monday, 48; Tuesday, 82; Wednesday, 94; Thursday, 81;
Friday 93; and on the Sabbath, 92. The Levitical choir had
a minimum of twelve male singers, from thirty to fifty
years old, with a minimum of five years of musical education. This rule dated back to the Davidic period when
the 288 "skillful singers" were divided into twenty-four
classes and taught music hereditarily thereafter. Boys were
allowed to join in the singing to add sweetness to the ma-
ture voices. However, to be a permanent member of the
chorus, a man was first required to devote twenty to thirty
years in training. Teaching music was an obligation as well

as a privilege, for we note that one leader of the Temple singers was remembered "in dishonor" because he refused to teach his special art to another. The Temple orchestra of the time consisted of two to six harps, nine or more lyres, two to twelve oboes, and one pair of cymbals; the orchestra of the first Temple (destroyed in 586 B.C.) consisted of similar instruments but lacked the oboes.

Instruments assumed an important role in the musical progress of the Hebrews. Instrumental music appears to have been an inherent part of the Temple service, and was employed, therefore, even on the Sabbath (refer to Sukkah 50 and 51). Vocal music did not hold the same status and could be omitted. Also, vocal music could be provided by anyone, while instrumental music fell strictly into the domain of the Levites, who played on all sacred occasions and particularly during the offering of sacrifices. The Bible specifically mentions some twenty-five or more instruments. Below are listed those most frequently mentioned

A. PERCUSSIVE INSTRUMENTS:

1) *Menaanaim—sistrum* or rattle, mentioned in II Samuel, concerning King David playing these before the Lord. Similar to the Egyptian type, with three or four crossbars in an inverted V-shaped frame with metal strips tied to the crossbars or pebbles hung onto them. Derived from the word meaning "to shake."

2) *Tziltzilim*—cymbals, usually of brass. Harsh cymbals in the Bible were called *tziltzile shma* and were heavy and struck vertically, while clear-sounding cymbals, called *tziltzile truah*, were lighter and struck horizontally, and were commonly used in

Palestine from 1100 B.C. An interesting story in the
tractate Sukkah of the Talmud deals with a pair of
brass cymbals which develops a crack, and, upon being
repaired, sounded worse than originally, whereupon
the repairs were removed and it sounded sweet once
more. A common type measured about five and one-
half inches in diameter and had holes in the center or
handles.

3) *Metziltayim*—clapper, mentioned in Chronicles,
Ezra, and Nehemiah thirteen times. May be similar
to cymbals, only smaller.

4) *Paamonim*—bells or jingles, used on priestly gar-
ments in defense against evil spirits.[43] On the robe of
the high priest, these were of gold and alternated with
golden pomegranates. They are now used for a decorative effect on the Torah scrolls.

5) *Tof*—generic name for drum, mentioned fifteen
times in the Old Testament, and always with a joyful
connotation. It is mentioned in connection with Saul
meeting the prophets, Miriam crossing the Red Sea,[44]
with David's procession before the Ark. It may have
been used in connection with wedding ceremonies,
for a passage in the Talmud refers to the drum as
erush, meaning "betrothed."

    a) Tambourine, timbrel or tabret—small hand
    drum of Egyptian origin with metal rings attached

---

43 Note the magical powers attributed to bells in several religions; in the
Sumerian legend, Nergal promises "to protect the singer of my deeds from
pestilence"—undoubtedly by means of the sacred bell; among medieval
Christians, churchbells were rung to ward off evil during a thunderstorm;
in Tibetan monasteries, bells were used in prayers for protection.

44 Edgerly suggests that Miriam may have been a dancing girl or a musician in
Egypt.

to its rim, usually round or oblong in shape (probably similar to Plate XXI).

b) Gourd drums—Egyptian type, some as long as two feet, covered with skin at the ends and braced with cords. Two slightly bent drumsticks were discovered with this type of instruments.

B. WIND INSTRUMENTS:

1) Pipes—[45]

a) *Halil*—a large flute or pipe reputed to have had a very sweet, oboe-like tone, used chiefly for elegiac purposes. It had a chromatic quality and was probably tuned in the following tetrachord: D, C♯, B♭, A, known as the Ahavah Rabbah mode. (See Appendix E.) This instrument was transmitted to the Greeks as the *mono-aulos* or *agathon*. Mentioned six times in the Bible, etymologists differ on the original root of the word, some saying that it is derived from the word meaning "pierced," while others associate it with the word "to dance" or the adjective "sweet." As a single instrument, Sachs refers to it as an oboe; when double, joined together at the mouthpiece or bound like panpipes, it is referred to as double oboe or double clarinet. Of the Egyptian single variety, most have five holes. The single flutes mentioned in the Talmud are made of metal or reed, the latter preferred by the Levites because

---

45 For various types of wind instruments, particularly pipes, common to this area, see Plates XIV and XV; the former, a Uganda *zomari* with four stops and deep V-notched mouthpiece; the latter, a Persian *sût*, the oldest type of flageolet or shepherd's pipe, of painted wood with six frontal and one dorsal stop.

of the sweeter tone elicited. The *halil* was played twelve days of the year before the altar in groups of two to twelve instruments. The Talmud classifies it with the *abuv*, and alludes to it as the instrument of noblemen. A story appears in the same source which tells of a *halil* of the Sanctuary from the days of Moses, which, when overlaid with gold, sounded harsh, so the gold was removed to restore the natural sweetness of the tones. The *halil* was used at the anointing of Solomon (I Kings, 1:40).

b) *Ugav*—general name applied to the organ, bagpipe, or flute. Used with the *halil* for weddings, funerals, and feasts. Mentioned four times in the Bible where the context shows the joyful nature of its usage. It stems from the word meaning "love" or "passion"; hence it was used to arouse the passions. Talmud, Sukkah, uses this in the sense of water organ.

c) *Abuv*—generally believed to be the flute, derived from the word meaning "hollow reed" or "bored," and known since the days of Moses. Probably, a pair of pierced pipes or an oboe in the modern sense, two to twelve of these were employed in the second Temple.

d) *Mashrokita*—double pipes or panpipes, similar to the Greek *syrinx* or *sarak*. Usually it had seven to thirteen reeds, and was of the type referred to as the shepherd's flute. It may also have been a small organ of seven pipes placed in a box with a mouthpiece for blowing.

e) *Shrika*—a whistle.

f) *Symphonia*—a bagpipe, the forerunner of the pipe-organ, and mentioned in Daniel 3:10. It may also have been a double flute with a single mouthpiece. Saadia, in the Talmud, calls it a shepherd's instrument, describing it in more detail as "an inflated skin, like the lung where the bronchial tubes enter it."[46] Sachs argues that this really refers to a type of antiphonal performance, referring to an orchestra where people hear first the single instrument, followed by a combination of all the instruments. The solo, thus, was followed by the remaining performers in antiphonal style.

g) *Magrepha*—an organ, from the root meaning "to shovel," "sweep away" or "grasp." Some authorities feel it refers to small organ pipes with hot-air pressure; others, to a water organ. Farmer, in *The Organ of the Ancients*, suggests the *ugav* of the Bible may mean the organ. Since the hydraulic organ originated about the fourth century B.C., early organs were probably pneumatic. Kirschner suggests that the *mashrokita* in Daniel 3:5, 7, 10, 15 was a pneumatic organ worked by hand. Both Talmuds describe the *magrepha* as giving the Levites their cue to begin the service, the Mishna remarking that this, plus oboes, cymbals, *shofars*, and singing, could be heard as far away as Jericho —a possibility in the still atmosphere of Jerusalem. One thousand different tones were possible on the *magrepha*, produced on ten pipes, each with

---

46 See Plate XVI for a similar type of instrument. This Algerian *zuqqâra* consists of a kidskin resonator, two cane tubes, cowhorn bells, and a single reed in the reservoir end of the pipes.

ten holes and with ten keys. Air was supplied by
two pairs of bellows, each twenty inches wide and
twenty inches high, operated by a protruding
handle.[47]

2) Horns:

a) *Keren*—generic name for the horn family, and
probably curved like the *shofar*.

b) *Shofar*—a ram's horn. Engel suggests it is a
derivation of the word meaning "bright," signifying a clear tone. Others say it comes from the
Assyrian word *sapparu*, meaning a ram. Mentioned seventy-two times in the Bible, it is the
only ancient instrument still in use in the synagogue. Only handled by priests, it is blown in
most communities today only for the New Year
or in time of danger. It was commonly used in
Biblical times to summon the people together or
to warn of impending danger. Zechariah 9:14, 15
suggests the idea of God blowing on it to fright-
en His enemies. After the second Temple, the
idea appertained to Elijah, who is to announce
the Redemption. Used on New Year's Day, its
sound is believed to remind God of His promise
to Abraham. Saadia Gaon (*circa* 900 of the
Christian Era) and Maimonides (1135-1204)
agree that its purpose is to move people to awe.
The Mishnah states that one *shofar* was to be
blown for the New Year and two for fast days

---

47 Plate XVII is a bronze reproduction of the pipes and air-chamber of a
hydraulis of Pompeii or Herculaneum. In this case, the air is supplied by
mechanical means with the aid of compressors and pistons.

in ancient times. Two types were in use in the
Temple, the curved (male) one with silver-cov-
ered mouthpiece for fast days, and the straight
(female) gold-mouthed type for the New Year.
Only the curved one is used today. Some say that
the straight one was used originally for Temple
service, while the curved type served a secular
purpose. The Talmud describes a New Year
shofar as the horn of an ibex or wild-goat, its
mouthpiece gold-inlaid. The crescent ram's horn
was used not only for fast days but for excom-
munications, as well as to announce death, to
frighten demons, to announce the New Moon, and
today, in Tel Aviv, to announce each week the
beginning of the Sabbath. Magical usages have
included felling the walls of Jericho by *shofar*
blasts, Gideon's midnight attack, which included
300 shofars to frighten his enemies, Zachariah's
description of God proclaiming Israel's salvation,
and, in Talmudic times, to drive out demons and
spirits, particularly in the story of the Dybbuk.
The fundamental idea underlying the power of
the *shofar* in particular and the power of music
in general in Semitic lore, is that sound may gov-
ern matter. The *shofar's* purpose is to remind man
of his sins and of the brevity of human life, according to the Talmud. Three types of blasts are
mentioned—the *t'kiah* is a pure sound signifying
man's first awakening to penitence and his sincere
resolve to keep his heart clean; *t'ruah*, used as a
danger signal; and *sh'varim*. Traditional *shofar*

blasts still used in the synagogue are described in the Talmud as follows: [48]

1) *T'kiah* (blast): appoggiatura on the tonic, prefixed to a long blow on the fifth.

2) *Sh'varim* (breaks): rapid alteration on tonic and fifth.

3) *T'ruah* (din): quavering blast on the tonic, ending on the fifth.

4) *T'kiah G'dolah* (great blast): long sostenuto on the tonic ending on the fifth.

The metrical length described is one *t'kiah*=three *t'ruahs*=nine *sh'varim*.

c) *Hatzozeroth*—a pair of silver trumpets used by the priests. Mentioned twenty-nine times in the Old Testament, it is also represented on the Arch of Titus at Rome. Accredited to Moses, it was used chiefly to frighten enemies and to call to God for help. It is said by Josephus to be twenty-one inches long, slightly wider than a flute, ending in a bell, similar to the Egyptian trumpet. (Figure F.)

d) *Sabeca* or *sambuca*—from *sak-buk*, meaning a sack-pipe. Authorities all differ on what type of instrument it was. Some say it was a type of trombone with sliding wooden tubes, while others identify it with the bagpipe mentioned in the

---

48 See Appendix E, 3, for the *Shofar* call. Also compare Plate XVIII, a traditional *shofar*, which has been steamed and flattened into shape, with Plate XIX, a more ornate and sophisticated descendant, a sixteenth-century English *oliphant* of ivory, bearing on it the head of Henry VIII, amidst hunting scenes.

Book of Daniel; still others associate it with the Greek *sambuca*, a small triangular harp of high pitch. Engel considers it a sort of guitar,[49] associating it with an Egyptian stringed instrument of this name, meaning a ship-ladder, triangular in shape.

C. STRINGS:

1) *Kinnor*—a cithara or lyre, mentioned forty-two times in the Old Testament and the favorite stringed instrument of Palestine, similar to the Greek *cithara*, but in the traditional shape of the *menorah* (candelabrum). It achieved fame as the instrument of King David, even to the extent of having many legends of magical powers associated with it. Legend claims that the word *kinnor* is connected with Lake Kinnereth in Galilee, since the fruits of the garden were said to be as sweet as the music of the *kinnor*. The earliest type possessed from three to twelve strings of sheepgut,[50] possibly a plectrum, and was held in a slanting position, crossbar at the top away from the player, while the left hand dampened the strings. The Babylonian type to follow held the crossbar at the bottom. In the Temple, sacred *kinnors* were not to have knotted or mended strings, but rather the broken string was to be shifted and reattached. The *kinnor* may be of

---

49 For further discussion, refer to Finesinger's article in the *Hebrew Union College Annual*, 1926, on "Musical Instruments of the Old Testament."

50 An interesting account in Kinnim 3:6, of the Talmud, deals with the fact that the live sheep emits one sound, while the dead animal emits seven sounds; its two horns become trumpets, its legs flutes, its skin a tambourine, its large intestine strings for a harp, its small intestine cithara strings.

Syrian origin, for it was mentioned in the Bible by Laban the Syrian who is said to have played it, and it can also be traced to the Syrian root "*kinroth*." Others believe it to have been brought from Egypt[51] about 1500 B.C., as it was similar to the Egyptian V-shaped lyre, which characteristically has a deep, full body of wood or tortoise-shell with branching horns joined by a wooden crossbar to prevent strings from loosening. The Hebrew ones were made of fir wood, berosh, almug, sandalwood, or even metal. Stainer suggests that *kinnor* melodies were gay, since the Israelites in Babylonia refused to play before their captors, although it is conceivable that Levite musicians would naturally refuse to play sacred melodies before a mocking conqueror. A further justification for the idea concerning the happy nature of the instrument can be traced to the threats of the prophets, chastening the people, and threatening that the *kinnor* be silent until the people desist from sin. (See Figure I for lyres.)

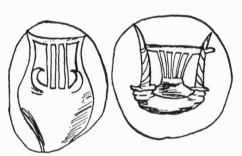

FIGURE I. HEBREW LYRES DEPICTED ON SECOND-CENTURY B.C. PALESTINIAN COINS

51 Probably similar to the Semitic lyre exhibited on an Egyptian wall painting at Beni-Hasan, and found on Plate XX.

2) *Nevel*—harp, mentioned twenty-seven times in the Bible, and probably a skin-covered harp or zither of twelve strings. It is regarded by some as a lute or a vertical, angular harp. Rabbi Joseph, in the Talmud, associated it with a skin-bottle (etymological meaning) because of its shape; or it may have been derived from a word meaning "dry" and referring to a gourd. Engel considers it akin to the Egyptian lute which was bottle- or gourd-shaped. Made of firewood or sandalwood it was frequently carried on the shoulder. The *nevel-asor* was a ten-stringed variant played with a plectrum. The Hebrews used both the Egyptian-type, bow-shaped, bottom-resonator harp and the Assyriantype, triangular, top-resonator harp, neither of which had a frontal pillar. The bow-shaped variety was much out of tune because of the flexibility of the bow. Since it was plucked with the fingers or plectrum, the word *zamer* (to pluck) is used in connection with this, while the word *nigen* (to play) is referred to the *kinnor*. Two to six of the *nevels* were commonly used in the Temple.

3) *Asor*—zither, consisted of ten strings and was similar to the Phoenician psaltery. It was probably rectangular and dated from about the eighth century B.C.

4) *Psanterin*—psaltery or dulcimer, consisted of twelve to twenty-one strings and a sounding board, and was plucked or struck with a short rod. It was mentioned in the story of David, and was regarded by Saadia as the equivalent of the *nevel*, by Miller as a type of harp, and by Stainer as an Assyrian dulcimer.

5) *Minim*—a generic term applying to members of the string family.

6) *Kithros*—a Greek-type *cithara* used in the Temple accompanied by two trumpets and one cymbal.

7) *Shalishim*—may have been either a triangular instrument or a three-stringed instrument, or a dance in triple-meter. Since the root of the word means "three," it could also have referred to a *sistrum* with three parallel bars.

8) *Mahaloth*—referred to either a double flute or was simply the term for dances.

9) *Alamoth*—Dr. Werner suggests its etymology may be Assyrian, from *halimu* meaning "wooden," referring to a double flute or relating to a small Greek pipe called *"elymos."* It may also refer to a high-pitched instrument, since the word in Hebrew refers to "maidens," or it may possibly refer to a particular mode.

10) *Sheminith*—may either mean an eight-stringed instrument, or it may be a musical notation to be played an octave lower or *al ottava.*

Again, the study of the literature of the Hebrews, as of the other Semitic nations, is of great value in determining the style and vocabulary of its music. Several terms exist in the Bible which indicate musical sounds. Many scholars have contemplated the mysterious headings of the Psalms and the frequent recurrence of the word "selah" with an eye to the possibility of proving that a musical notation exists in these words. However, while we cannot prove that an inherent musical notation lies within these phrases, we do know that some terms, such as *higgaion* (solemn tone), *hol* (joyful sound), and *jovel* (loud, cheerful blast on the trumpet) indicate a musical vocabulary.[52] We do know, however, that certain words in the Psalms determined the style of the musical phrases. *Amens* and *hallelujahs* formed congregational responses. The audience participated in three types of alternation in the singing of the Psalms: (1) the answering refrain in such endings as "for His mercy endureth forever"; (2) the repetition of half-verses; and (3) true responsorial antiphony. We may draw some conclusions concerning the mood of the Psalms from the heading keyword, for headings probably indicated the mode or folk-tune to which a particular Psalm was to be sung.[53] For instance, the six *n'ginoth*

---

52 Note that in later times, *bar dahi* was the Hebrew term for a musician. Bard, of Celtic origin, may possibly be traced to this, since Hebrew singers and performers roved abroad like the troubadours of the Middle Ages. The term may even be associated with the *bhat,* the bard of India.

53 Below is a list of several Psalm-headings and the possible meanings which may be illustrative of the mood of the Psalm or, a further possibility, the name of the popular tune to which it was sung:

Lamnatzeah—to be performed, or, to the chief conductor.

Neginah—a stringed instrument.

Nahaloth—musical instrument or flute.

Sheminith—eighth.

Gittit—wine-press, or from the town of Gath.

Mut laben—die-white, or son's death.

Shoshanim—lilies.

Alamoth—maidens.

Ayeloth hashahar—hinds of dawn.

Jeduthun—confessors.

Mahaloth—diseases, or dances.

Yonath ilam rehakim—far-off mute dove.

Shoshan-eduth—testimony of the lily.

Maskil—didactic poem.

Mihtam—epigrammatic poem.

Al-tashhit—destroy it not. (This may signify the melody of a popular drinking-song, its title a quotation from Isaiah 65:8, "Destroy it (the grape) not, for it is full of blessing.")

Psalms (4, 54, 55, 61, 67, 74) are prayers for escape, the three *gittit* ones (8,81,84) are gay, and the three *jeduthun* (39, 62, 77) show resignation. We may also conclude that the manner in which the particular Psalm was sung was partly, if not largely, dependent on its place in the Temple ritual. The Talmud, in describing psalm-singing in the service, speaks of the accompanying instruments and the rituals: a sign to begin was given on the cymbals, where-upon twelve Levites, standing on the steps of the stairway, leading from the congregation to the outer court of the priests, commenced to sing and accompany themselves on nine lyres, two harps, and a cymbal, while the priests poured out wine-offerings. A pause in the Psalm was usual-ly indicated by a trumpet blast of the priests on the right, and a cymbal clashing on the left. The oft-discussed word *selah* may have been the musical indication for this pause, which may have marked a cadence or a modulation.

We know that the Hebrews had a definite system of music, but we do not know actually the sounds of their music, although fragments of ancient Hebrew melodies have come down to us in modern synagogual chants, in Gregorian chant, and in the melodies of Yemen, Tunisia, and the Isle of Djerba. Melodies were not noted, but were transmitted from generation to generation. Idelsohn found exact counterparts of Gregorian chants in remote Jewish congregations in Yemen, Babylonia, and Persia, which may have existed in Palestine before 600 B.C., since these communities were disconnected from the homeland fol-lowing the destruction of the first Temple in 597 B.C.

In Biblical times, musical style was divided into two periods of evolution: from the second millennium B.C., it consisted of a vocal, Bedouin style, and from the first millennium B.C., it developed into a highly evolved instrumental, ecclesiastical style, with specific schools for the training of musicians. Two distinct styles of singing prevailed; the first, females singing accompanied by dancing and timbrel playing, is a style which exists today in Yemen and Tunisia.[54] The melody is symmetrical, repetitious, and very clear structurally. Drums and cymbals alternate with solo and chorus. It is not dependent on the text, but rather on motion: a periodical up and down movement, and falling on each period of the melody. The second style is performed by men or, occasionally, mixed groups, and was chiefly ecclesiastical, consisting of responses and antiphony with free meters and structural patterns. This was the music of the prophets, dynamic and expressionistic. The "falling of time" in this type of music can be traced to the early musical meters which arise from or are connected with the dance. This heritage was best preserved in the liturgy of the Oriental Jews in the Middle East, who permitted no variation of sacred music in the synagogue, leaving all music vocal and unaccompanied.[55] All liturgies demanded sweet singing, neither nasal nor loud, for the Talmud scorns those who read the Scriptures without melody, or study its words without singing. The service, based on the reading of the Bible, was melodious with alternation between cantor and congregation. The Psalms, even after being assigned definite places in the rigidly organized liturgy, probably retained the standard melodies and folk-tunes to which they had previously been

54 See Robert Lachmann's *Jewish Cantillation and Song on the Isle of Djerba.*
55 In early times, however, accompaniment and singing were inseparable. Note that the Babylonian captives would not sing, for their harps hung upon the willows. Also, in Chronicles, the lyre and the harp are called *k'le shir,* "instruments of song."

sung. Later cantillations developed from line patterns into word-motifs, ready-made as it were, which changed from word to word. This modern form of synagogual chant, based on sequence and variation of tones, upon the symmetrical structure of sentences, formed a mosaic pattern of composition, called *trope*.[56]

At the nomadic stage, there was little difference in style and melody between the tune of the shepherd and the prayers of the group: a fluent, continuous melody was characteristic, ranging from four to six tones in a recurring formula. After the return from Egypt, the music of the Israelites assumed a more definite shape under the influence of a foreign culture. Source materials demonstrating this change are to be found in Biblical narrative, in the poetry which followed this period, and in the mention of new instruments. In Egypt, the art of composing in modes developed into a system. The performer of ancient times composed a melody by arranging and combining a limited number of motives. The Oriental mind thinks in melodic formulae and tonal groups; there is no significance to a note out of its context. Hence, in the Orient, the word "to compose" has the true Latin meaning of "to put together." Thus, the systematization of Egyptian music may have become the fundamentals of Hebrew musical theory. Liturgy developed from certain modes and motives assigned to the reading of different portions of the Pentateuch, Prophets, Psalms, Song of Songs, and the Books of Ruth, Esther, Lamentations, and to the prayers. While Greek modes and scales assumed ethical and moral qualities, the Hebrew modes, eventually completely assimilated into the liturgy, became religious cult objects.

---

56 One of the foremost authorities on *trope* is Professor Solomon Rosowsky of Jerusalem.

While notation in Egypt was employed as far back as the twenty-eighth century B.C. but limited to hand and finger motions in order to remind performers of the notes, the Hebrews developed one of the earliest written musical notations which was superimposed over the text. No doubt, in periods of upheaval, when the Oral Tradition was in danger of being forgotten, the scholars, in their determination that the sacred texts and melodies be remembered accurately, wrote signs in the text to help both vowelization and singing.

One of the chief contributions that the Hebrews made to the musical world has been in the extensive use of antiphony, the musical associate of poetic parallelism in the Bible. Numerous examples exist which derive their poetic sense and rhythmic impulse from this dual stylization. Aside from the most famous poetic works in the Psalms, parallelism can be discovered in all Biblical poetry, from the earliest poem (Genesis 4:23)—

> *Adah and Zillah, hear my voice,*
> *Ye wives of Lamech, hearken unto my speech,*
> *For I have slain a man for wounding me,*
> *A young man for bruising me . . .*
> *If Cain shall be avenged sevenfold,*
> *Truly Lamech seventy and sevenfold*

to as late a book as that of the prophet Joel—

> *Hear this, ye old men,*
> *And give ear, all ye inhabitants of the land.*
> *Hath this been in your days,*
> *Or in the days of your fathers? . . .*

Musical antiphony developed from this poetic parallelism in the alternate singing of the two parallel lines by two half-choruses, or in the alternate singing of a soloist and the answering chorus. In the schools of the Temple days and later, children repeated the teacher's instructions in melodic half-verse repetition. Confirming refrains were used as early as the period of Moses (Deuteronomy 27:21-26, ending with "and all the people shall say Amen"). Antiphonal singing, accompanied by drums, clapping and dancing, is not only common today in such places as Yemen and North Africa, but has always been a universal form of music from Libya to Mesopotamia. Further, it is conceivable that antiphony, when accidentally overlapping, can be held responsible for producing the earliest form of real harmony and canonic style, which have undoubtedly been the influencing and differentiating factors in Western music.

CHAPTER IV

ARABIA:

CENTER OF MYRIAD INFLUENCES

ARABIA LIES BETWEEN AFRICA AND ASIA, NEAR THE CON-
quering Persians and Assyrians, next to the dynasts of
Egypt, and not far from the ancient wisdom of China and
India. All of these influences have undoubtedly fused in
the Arabian melting pot. Yet, there is so little known about
early Arabic music that few authorities risk mention of it.
It is known that during the period of the Israelites' musical
and cultural Golden Age (in the Temple days), the Arabs
were mainly a wild, scattered group of nomads possessing
few visible signs of culture. The foremost incentive in
creating a culture, that of bearing ties with a specific soil,
had not yet touched them. Nor had any of the duties

incumbent on a member of a civilized group, nor any of the pleasures of a sense of home and security reached the nomad who wandered the Arabian peninsula in search of sustenance. A man fought anyone outside of his own tribe, and, when his tribe or family could no longer offer him the necessities for survival, he fought them, too.

Yet we know that the Arabs were a musical people. While the music of the Hebrews had begun to crystallize into secular as well as ritualistic patternization, the Arabs remained in a primitive state of highly individualized, secular music. In fact, they remained more or less so until the time of Mohammed (630 of the Christian Era), when their culture and art developed so rapidly as to become immediately influential throughout Europe and North Africa. This period of Arabian ascendancy on the horizon of world art was a glorious one, for the Arabs rapidly developed fine art and poetry distinguished by a delicate sense of balance and detail, handicrafts such as weaving and ceramics unsurpassed for beauty of decorative style, the art of calligraphy heretofore developed only by the Far East, and the arts of music and singing at the dazzling court of Harun al-Rashid. But even in the early days, with which we are chiefly concerned, the Arabs possessed beauty in their songs and an amazing assortment of instruments. Arab legend credits Jubal of the Bible, descendant of Cain, with the first song, an elegy on the death of Abel. Lamech was supposed to have been the inventor of the lute, and his son, Jubal-cain, of the drum and tambourine. The daughters of Cain were the first musicians and inventors of instruments, legend says;[57] and today in Arabia

---

57 According to Bar Hebraeus of the Christian Era of the thirteenth century.

a singing girl is called a *Kaina*. Women, however, were not of equal standing as musicians among the Arabs, and were completely banned from religious music.

Edgerly[58] says that there are more than 120 different kinds of Arabian instruments known today of which at least half were known from ancient days, many of these the forerunners of modern instruments. Thirty-two varieties of lutes were commonly known, twelve of *kanoons*, fourteen of bowed instruments, three of lyres, twenty-eight of flutes, twenty-two of oboes, eight of trumpets, and a limitless number of drums. Below are listed several of the more popular musical instruments:

A. PERCUSSION:
   1) Bells—used with drums in battle.
   2) Drums—various types existed. Kettledrums had copper bodies and parchment heads (like our own today). Originally they were bound to the player and played with a strip of camel's hair between the fingers of one hand. Also snare drums, square drums, *doff*, and tambourine-shaped drums existed.
   3) Tambourine—called *târ*, is found in Plate XXI. Note the disk jigglers and the membrane glued to the top. It is used throughout Islam, Europe, Africa, and Asia even today.

B. WIND INSTRUMENTS:
   1) Organ—supposed to have originated in Arabia, the pneumatic organ was known in early times, although the first description we have of it is on the

---

58 Edgerly, B., "From the Hunter's Bow," p. 89.

obelisk at Istanbul, erected by Theodosius in the fourth century of the Christian Era. The instrument had eight pipes and required two boys to pump air into it with clumsy bellows.

2) Flute—called *gosba* or *djaouack*, was used to accompany dances. Blowing in long difficult passages of trills and slides was accomplished by breathing through the nose to prevent interruption of blowing. Reed as well as bamboo flutes were used, played vertically.

3) Oboe, or *zamir*—was a favorite instrument.

4) Trumpet—of buffalo horn or shell. Two types were popular: the *nefer*, a war trumpet with bell and mouthpiece, and the *raita*, a kind of musette. In Plate XXII we see an *al gaita* from Nigeria in Hausa. Note the conical bore and the five frontal stops. The metal lip-disk in the reed tube is missing. This is related to the Islamic *zamir* and trumpet, and known today in Morocco as *el ghaida*.

5) Bagpipe—compare the native type (Figure J) with the *zuqqâra* on Plate XVI.

FIGURE J. ARABIAN BAGPIPE (GAJDA)

C. Strings:

1) Lute—of the stringed instruments, all of which were very popular, this was a favorite. Named *el oud*, signifying the wood from which it was constructed, it had from four to eight strings, and a very narrow neck about a yard long.[59] *Mandore, pandore,* and guitar were its later developments.[60] *Saz* was a similar instrument, very slender of neck with an accentuated double body. Similarly, the bass-stringed *sharode* which was its descendant, designed by a tenth-century philosopher of Bagdad, was shaped like a violin with a deeply spacious body. The *guenbei* was of the same family, delicately pear-shaped, painted and decorated, having two or three strings. Many of these instruments were richly inlaid with beautiful woods, shell, or ivory. (In Plate XXIV an unusual figure-8-shaped lute or *tar* from Tiflis is shown, possessing movable gut frets and a parchment soundboard.)

2) *Kemângeh-a-gûz*—one of several types of bowed instruments. Its body was of cocoanut shell or gourd with a long, gracefully tapering neck of ebony inlay. It had two to four strings, and a rod of wood supported its tiny body on the ground, while the performer sat crosslegged, sawing with a bow (of Persian

---

59 See Plate XXIII for the Turkish *al'ud,* an eleven-stringed lute, in which the lower strings are tuned in five pairs, with a single upper melody string. Note the three beautifully carved rosette soundholes and the tortoise-shell guard over the wood to protect it from the plectrum. The backward bent pegbox was later abandoned in Europe.

60 Popular in later days from Borneo to Europe, the *mandore* was derived from a tapering-necked instrument with a sickle-shaped pegbox, and later called the "Moorish guitar" or "bowed *rebâb.*" The mandolin is derived from the *pandore.*

origin) as long as the instrument itself. (Plate XXV illustrates a *kemânǧeh* with a daintily painted cocoa-nut resonator and movable spike below this to shift the height of the instrument when playing vertically.)

3) *Rebâb*—similar to a mandolin, in early times possessing two gut strings, plucked with fingers or with a crude plectrum, and having a range of six notes. It was played in later days with a bow. Later known as a *rebeck*, in Renaissance times it was associated with the French *gigue* dance. (Plate XXVI is a *rebâb* from Java, similar to the Arabian type. A folded banana skin was placed under the bridge to remove the harsh tone. Resin was placed on the body near the neck and was scraped by the bow while playing.)

4) *Kanoon*—zither or dulcimer, which had as many as seventy-five strings, stretched over dry skins on a box-frame, forming a rectangular resonating chamber. Plucked with a quill or ivory plectrum, it was called also a *psalter* and was the ancestor of the clavichord and spinet. (See Figure K.)

FIGURE K. KANOON

FIGURE L. KESSAR

(5 *Santir*—another ancestor of the piano, originated possibly from the Hebrew or Assyrian *asor*. Usually two feet long by one foot wide, it had a wooden frame as a sounding board, generally covered with skins, and

hung from the neck. Struck either with a plectrum or with wooden hammers, it was associated with the Greek psalter which predated the organ (200 B.C.).

6) Lyre or *kessar*—was retained in simple form as was the harp, a five-stringed instrument of tortoise shell and wood. (See Figure L.)

The Arabs, unlike the Hebrews, have left us a generous amount of data concerning their compositions. They had countless modes and scales,[61] and unlike many early peoples, possessed certain established modes of singing and playing before they had a religion. Arabic scales were supposed to have been developed largely from lute playing. Zalzal (1100 B.C.), a gifted performer, is reputed to have noticed that in playing the lute, the middle finger had no use, so he tied a string between two others, thereby adding two more tones to the lute scale which formed the "usual" Arabic scale.[62]

Many types of songs were created by the Arabs, the popular European serenade being one in particular. Throughout its performance, the accompanist interspersed a display of technique consisting in the main of arpeggios and pizzicati. Most Arabic songs possessed a folk character, evident in very short phrases and in the expression of rhythmical, rather than scale, construction. This may have been due to the fact that veritably all transmission from early times had been oral, and it was undoubtedly easier to remember such song forms rather than complex ones. The

---

61 See Appendix E for several Arabic modes.

62 Smith, *The World's Earliest Music*, p. 22. What is meant by "usual" scale is unknown, since some three or four scales were used regularly as well as some ten others which were fairly common.

most compound form of Arabic song known is the *bashraw* which is in rondo form, following the alternating scheme of first, second and third themes: A B A C A. The lack of notation, which made it necessary to learn songs by rote, gave rise to the use of embellishments, such as trills, mordants, and appoggiaturas, *ad libitum*. In time, all Arabic composition became merely an arrangement, transition, and embellishment of motives, or *makimim* of a certain scale. Different types of motives arose: conjunctive, disjunctive, etc., characterizing the modes they formed. All instruments played in unison while a continual rhythmic drumbeat accompanied them; sustained tones were avoided unless accompanied by a tremolo. Two general types of modes were (1) the *tartil*, unrhythmical recitative which was favored among the Arabs and accompanied by a lyre or *kanoon*, continually repeating the melodic line with variations; and (2) the *aushada*, a less frequently used dance-like, rhythmic mode.

Tonality consisted of quarter tones; hence, the octave contained twenty-four steps. An octave (*jewab*) was usually built on tetrachordal or pentachordal lines. The most popular tetrachord was called *hejaz* and consisted of the tones A, F♯, E♭, D. Arabic scales formed the bulk of Greek composition in later days. It is of interest to note that most Hebrew as well as Arabic songs were based on the four modes shown in Appendix E.[63] In the Orient, these scales based upon quarter tones are still used, although the West employs some of these scales within the framework of a half-tone system.

Meter was extremely significant and stylized in Arabian

---

63 In Appendix E, the similarity between Arabic, Greek, and Hebrew scales is illustrated.

music. Specific meters were employed for typical moods and musical forms, often with a monotone vocal and drum accompaniment.[64] Meter, probably from earliest times, consisted of accents in timbre rather than force. Most ancient tongues, including Chinese, make themselves understood more clearly by inflection rather than by actual word. Thus, it is not surprising to find that even in the later (Moslem) Arabic period, rhythmic beats were indicated by *dum*, representing a muffled beat (piano), *dim*, a less muffled one (mezzo-piano), and *tak*, a clear or accented beat (forte), with *tik*, a less clear beat (mezzo-forte).

In the nomadic period, only men were permitted to be musicians, while during the Caliphate, women of the palace were extensively employed and trained for this purpose. Farmer[65] suggests that several instruments, particularly the organ, were played by a debased class of men; hence, the social status of the musician was not as high as it had been in Palestine, Egypt, and Mesopotamia. However, the Arabs of the Mohammedan period wrote sound musical treatises, and seemed to hold in veneration all music, from the complicated instrumental modes to the simple *muezzin* call, which they transmitted through a period of 1300 years. And contradicting this further, was it not an Arab who said: "He who hunts not, loves not, trembles not with the tones of music, is no man"?

---

64 Also the eight characteristic meters are shown in Appendix D.
65 Farmer, *The Organ of the Ancients*, p. 6.

CHAPTER V

ASSYRIA:

OUTSIDE THE SUMERO-AKKADIAN CULTURE

ASSYRIA LIES TO THE NORTH OF THE SUMERO-AKKADIAN world. In the ruins of Assur, its first capital, many valuable texts and statues were uncovered, disclosing a highly developed civilization outside the sphere of Sumero-Akkadian culture. Statuary reveals that this was one of the early groups to be known for their profuse beards; indeed, to the smooth-skinned, carefully shaven Egyptian, the Assyrian must have looked every bit of a barbarian. In the *Annals of the Kings of Assyria*, discovered in Assur, such great names appear as that of Shalmaneser I (*circa* 1290-1260 B.C.), who conquered neighboring tribes and moved his boundaries toward Mesopotamia; Tiglath Pileser

I (*circa* 1115-1110 B.C.), who extended his dominion to the Mediterranean; Shalmaneser II whose obelisk, now in the British Museum, shows him receiving tribute from Jehu, King of Israel; Sargon II (*circa* 722-705 B.C.), who defeated the Israelites and other peoples and whose son, Sennacherib, is mentioned in Biblical accounts. Thirty years after the *Annals* break off (636 B.C.), Assyria was completely destroyed by the Medes.

In Assyria, as in Egypt, the god (Ashur, in this case) was the true master of the land through his priests, while the king was only a vice-regent, receiving his orders from the deity. The people were divided into two classes: free men and slaves. Family life was highly revered, for even slave families were never separated. Monogamy ruled, even among slaves, although concubinage was occasionally permitted. The legal age for marriage was ten years. Slaves could rise to power if possessed of exceptional ability (note the case of a slave of the queen who rose to the position of inspector of cities). Much money went into the maintenance of a standing army. Assyria gave us the use of chariots and horses for warfare, as well as other constructive contributions, such as biennial rotation of crops, building of aqueducts, and cultivation of cotton. The peoples they conquered they enslaved and deported while razing their cities to the ground. In fact the Assyrians were renowned for their love of battle and cruelty to captives.

The art of Assyria consisted chiefly of architecture and metallurgy. Kings built many temples studded with bas-reliefs. Palaces contained courts, kitchens, bakeries, communicating rooms, reception rooms, and private apartments. Inlays and tiles were favored in the construction of buildings, and enameled and plain brick were often used, while asphalt was placed under pavements and at the bottom of drains. Main gates were frequently ornamented and encased in precious metal. The Assyrians achieved renown, too, for their beautiful fabrics, ofttimes regally embroidered with gold threads. Fine cotton as well as silken robes were manufactured.

In human sculpture, the Assyrians concentrated on clothing and ornamentation, and achieved perfection in animal representations. In the eighth century B.C., a conscious effort was made to isolate figures from the background, to enlarge proportions and to suppress accessories. In military scenes, landscapes are clearly delineated, while in hunting scenes, the background is dropped in order to focus on the figures (note the magnificent lion transfixed by an arrow, in the British Museum). Chiseling grew more accurate as a new style of grouped figures in tiers achieved popularity. The human figures rarely exhibited distinctive individual or racial features, and were always shown strictly in profile. Paints were used only to emphasize detail: only black, white, red, blue, and rarely green were used. The Assyrians were famous for a rich shade of vermilion which they used commonly, and which can still be seen on bas-reliefs of Assyrian palaces. Mention is made in Ezekiel 23:14 of the "images of the Chaldeans portrayed with vermilion." Tables were a frequent accessory in sculptured scenes, for the belief was that they drove away demons, and furniture generally was an important part of life and very luxurious, with seats and tables heavily decorated. Metal vases imported from Phoenicia, ivory objects from Egypt, and native glass and stone pottery abounded.

Occasional cylinder and flat seals have been found.

Historical documents include war texts chiefly used to glorify royal conquests, while some epistolatory literature exists along with magical texts. On the whole, the literature and science of Assyria were similar to those of Babylonia.

The poetry of Assyria had much in common with that of Egypt and Palestine. Parallelism again was a common feature, as in the "Hymn to the God Sin," quoted below.

> *O Lord who is like thee?*
> *Who can be compared to thee?*
> *Mighty One, who is like thee?*
> *Who can be compared to thee?*

The Assyrians had several varieties of musical instruments, many portrayed on plinth decorations. Great numbers of players and singers were used in ceremonial processions, stamping and clapping to the rhythmic beat. Musicianship was highly esteemed in early times, and of all war captives, musicians alone were spared. On the walls of Sennacherib's palace at Kouyunjik were famous carvings of processions greeting victorious generals on their return from wars, dating from about 700 B.C. One such wall painting depicts a procession of instrumental and vocal performers to meet the returning conquerors. Seven harps, two double pipes, one dulcimer, and one drum were played, accompanied by a chorus of females and children singing, clapping, and dancing in time to the music.

The following instruments were played by the Assyrians:

A. PERCUSSION INSTRUMENTS:

1) Cymbals—used chiefly in dance rhythms, from two and a half to five and a half inches in diameter, and of copper with holes for handles. For another type, see Figure M.

FIGURE M. ASSYRIAN CYMBALS

2) Castanets and tambourines.
3) Bells—used to adorn horses' necks.
4) Drums—*tubbul*, a large drum beaten at both ends and suspended from a belt. Also small cylindrical or thimble-shaped drums were played vertically in war, being bound to the body of the performer. Only the upper part was covered with skin, and was always beaten by hand.

B. WIND INSTRUMENTS:

1) Flute—usually of clay with two fingerholes and blown at the ends. Also double flutes (*malileo*) were played by both sexes. At Birsi Nimrud (and now in the Museum of the Royal Asiatic Society) what is possibly the oldest clay flute was discovered, still well preserved. Three inches long, it consists of a mouthpiece and two fingerholes, yielding the follow-

ing approximate tones: both closed—C; left open—E
flat; right open—E natural; both open—G. Hence,
we have here a major or minor triad. Other tones may
be obtained by overblowing. Notice the shape, possibly in the form of an animal's head, and see Figures
N and O.

FIGURE N. CLAY FLUTE

FIGURE O. ASSYRIAN SINGLE
PIPE OR VERTICAL FLUTE

2) Panpipes—usually clay and bound together.
3) Oboe—called *zunai*, and played together with the
drum. Also a *passu*, or double reed oboe, was used in
martial display and its tone was considered an incentive to bravery. It is frequently displayed in bas-
reliefs.
4) Bagpipe—a one-piece instrument.
5) Trumpet—ever-present with drums in battle, and
made of the simplest type of metal horn used for calling orders and announcements.
6) Conch or shell-horn—an instrument of high

antiquity and connected with religious rites. A speci-
men from the ruins of Nineveh is preserved in the
British Museum.

C. STRINGED INSTRUMENTS:
1) *Tamboura* or lute—similar to the Egyptian *nefer*,
called *sinnitu*, and found on an eighth-century tablet.
2) Dulcimer or zither or *santir* type of instrument.
3) Harp—frequently triangular in shape with a top
resonator. One harp was discovered, its frame four
feet high with vertical strings, which may have been
played while marching. The sounding holes had an
odd hourglass shape, and the strings may have been
of silk (like the Burmese instrument) or of catgut
(like the Egyptian). Strings numbered from three to
twenty-two. A horizontal type (Figure P) was called

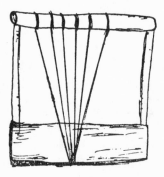

FIGURE P. ASSYRIAN
HORIZONTAL HARP (*c.* 650 B.C.)

FIGURE Q. ASSYRIAN LYRE

eširtu, and may be compared with the dulcimer on
Plate IX.
4) Lyre—the small rectangular type was fairly com-

mon (see Figure Q) although angular and curved
ones were known. The Nubian lyre (similar to the
Arabian *kessar*) is believed to be related to the Assyrian lyre. Of a square or circular body, the Nubian
lyre was made of wood and covered with sheepskin,
containing three closely placed sounding holes, a
wooden bridge to lift the five strings which were
frequently made of camel's intestines. A plectrum of
horn or leather was attached by a cord.

5) *Sambuca*—an early stringed instrument, possibly
related to the *sabeca* of the Hebrews.

Sir Henry Layard, who restored the ruins of Assyria
for the British Museum, gives an interesting description of
a panel depicting fifty-two musicians:

"Assyrian generals were welcomed by bands of men
and women, dancing, singing, and playing on instruments.
First came five men, three carrying harps which they
struck with both hands, dancing to the measure; the fourth
playing double pipes similar to those shown on Egyptian
monuments. A fifth musician carried an instrument consisting of a number of strings stretched over a hollow case
or sounding board (*santir*). The strings, pressed with the
fingers of the left hand to produce notes, were struck with
a wand held in the right hand. The men were followed
by six female musicians, four playing on harps, one on a
double pipe and one on a kind of drum beaten with both
hands (*tubbul*). The musicians were accompanied by six
women and nine boys and girls of different ages, singing
and clapping in rhythm. The first were distinguished by
various headdresses. Some wore hair in large ringlets,
others plaited, braided, or confined in a net. One woman

held her hands to her throat as do the Arab and Persian women when making the shrill vibrating sounds peculiar to the vocal music of the East. The musicians portrayed were of a class of public performers appearing today in Turkey and Egypt at marriages and other festive occasions."

Evidently, vocal music was characteristically important while instrumental music was more subdued. The small number of percussion instruments may be considered a sign of refinement. Undoubtedly, Assyrian hymns were sung in the fashion of other vocal Semitic music, with refrains in which the congregation joined, and with antiphonal responses between leader and choir, and between the separate choirs themselves. This type of singing and these instruments, more or less universal from Mesopotamia to the Mediterranean, were to wield a powerful influence on the music of the Greeks.

CHAPTER VI

PHOENICIA:

WHERE MUSIC STRESSED THE SENSUAL

LITTLE IS KNOWN CONCERNING THE MUSIC OR CULTURE OF
the Phoenicians who inhabited that section of land north
of Palestine. Probably most of the culture of this people
was derived from or entwined with those nations with
whom they traded. The Phoenicians were known as a seafaring, mercantile people, who developed an alphabet of
separate letters instead of ideographic symbols and, in their
extensive traveling and colonization, helped to spread this
alphabet. They were believed to have been influenced cul-
turally by Babylonia, Egypt, and Assyria, and they gave
much to the Greeks, who borrowed through them Semitic
instruments and musical theory. Great builders and fine

95

architects, they developed the foundations of the arch in architecture in the use of carved rock, and built sturdy and beautiful pillars (the gift of twin pillars, Boaz and Jachin, to Solomon for building the Temple). Phoenician art shows the influence of the Hittites and the Mesopotamians. Just as the bull was the favorite animal of Egypt, so the lion was used for ornamental purposes in Phoenicia. Sculpture remained relatively crude because of the lack of marble or other smooth rock which might be carved. The pock-marked native limestone was so filled with fossil shells as to make it unworkable; hence, a smoother lime-stone was regularly imported from Cyprus. Statues were beautifully curved and draped,[65a] but were meant to be seen only from the front, since the sides and back were left unfinished. Figures, as a rule, were completely draped, although their naturally stiff attitudes were relieved some-what by smiling faces.

Geometrical patterns were much to the tastes of the Phoenicians. We admire their ornately but delicately worked jewelry, their fine ivory carvings, mosaic pave-ments in temples, exquisite bronze-embossed dishes and beautifully dyed fabrics (from earliest times Tyrian purple received world recognition). Ships, because of the people's seafaring inclinations, were carved with loving care upon wall plaques, and were a favorite form of design.

The musical instruments and music illustrated the affinity of culture between Phoenicia and Palestine. Pro-fessional musicians enjoyed the same position in society as the priests, and were permitted to wear a skullcap as a sign of their profession.

65a A uniquely graceful fish-tail skirt of draperies adorns a statue on a Cartha-ginian sarcophagus.

Unlike the severely religious orchestras of the Hebrews, which were subject to laws aiming to elevate their purpose, the Phoenician orchestras had a purely sensual purpose: to express extremes of passionate joy or deep lamentation. Instruments, like the pipes, were used to lament the death of Adonis, while others, such as double pipes, cymbals, and drums, are described by Lucien as having been used in the spring Ishtar-festival to stimulate the youth to a frenzied sexual craze. A general listing of Phoenician instruments would include:

1) Flute—called *ababas*, it was similar to the Hebrew *ugav*. Also the *gingra* was a small flute used primarily for accompanying dances. Both of these instruments had an affinity to the worship of the goddess Ishtar and the god Tammuz. A later name of the goddess was Gingira.

2) Double flute—usually played with leather facial supports, similar to the Greek manner. (See double flute on Figure R.)

Figure R. Phoenician Psaltery, Timbrel, and Double Pipe; from Ivory Box; *c.* 800 b.c.

3) Psaltery or zither—usually square-shaped with ten strings (Figure R).

4) *Nabla* or *nevel*—a vertical, angular harp, with twelve strings and plectrum used.

5) *Kinnor or* lyre—triangular in form, and used to accompany hymns, prayers, chants and processionals.

6) Timbrel and percussions. (See Figure R.)

CHAPTER VII

SYRIA:

SHAPER OF ARMENIAN CHURCH MUSIC

THE MUSIC OF SYRIA (ALSO REFERRED TO IN THE BIBLE AS Aram) was connected, in the main, with the planetary system, a fact proving some connection to have existed between the cultures of Egypt and Syria.[66] Relatively little is known about the culture of early Syria beyond the fact that music played an important role in the life of the

---

66 Hitti, in his *History of Syria,* suggests that there may have been more than a casual relationship between Syria and Egypt. Syrian girls were prized in Egypt, and undoubtedly were a factor in transmitting some cultural elements from the one group to the other. Glaze painting is believed to have reached Egypt from northern Syria, as well as the custom of affixing tassels to lutes and the use of lyres, which first appeared among Semitic Bedouins of the Twelfth Dynasty. See Plate XX.

people. Musicians were respected and, when captured in battle, were spared and cared for. We are told[67] that victors were regularly greeted by rows of musicians playing such instruments as harps, double pipes, and drums, while women and children followed, singing and clapping. A bas-relief from the Kouyunjik palace (and now in the British Museum) illustrates such a victorious procession. Among the instruments commonly used by the Syrians (many of them borrowed from their Semitic neighbors) are:

1) Harps—all stringed instruments were greatly favored; therefore, these came in a variety of sizes, from a small hand-harp to a giant of seven-foot size. Resembling the harps of the Phoenicians in that they possessed no frontal pillar, they were triangular in shape, and the strings were plucked by hand or with a plectrum of ivory or wood. Made of light-weight materials so as to be carried without difficulty while dancing, these were later given soundholes and used in conjunction with other stringed instruments, pipes, flutes, and bagpipes.

2) Lyres—of various sizes and shapes.

3) *Tamboura*—a lute, similar to the Egyptian *nefer*, pictured on sculpture at El Amarna (*circa* 1375 B.C.). One such instrument, ten-stringed and three-feet high, is inlaid with mother-of-pearl.

4) *Sambuca*—similar to that of Assyria.

5) Pipes—bound like panpipes.

6) Flutes—single or double, of clay.

---

67 Edgerly, B., *From the Hunter's Bow,* page 81.

7) Bagpipes.

8) Trumpets—of metal, used with drums for warfare. (Refer to Plate XXVII for an unusual poly-globular-shaped trumpet from Damascus.)

9) Drums—light and small, used for warfare. (See Figure S.)

10) Castanets—used with cymbals to accompany dancing.

11) Cymbals—used primarily for dancing.

12) Bells—very rare; of fine metal and used to decorate horses.

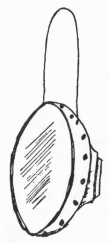

FIGURE S. SYRIAN DRUM (Tabil Šamî)

Vocal music in Syria had its identifying characteristics. When a syllable ended in a consonant, the value of the preceding vowel tone was doubled. A sign frequently appeared in texts and manuscripts resembling an exclamation point (!) which meant to inhale deeply and to sing the following passage an octave lower. Reference is made to

a tetrachordal structure showing an association with Hebrew melody. Alternating long and short tones, and an
elaborate antiphony in half-chorus against chorus or soloist
are other characteristics of this type of music. Ancient
Syria was one day to shape the cantillation for the Ar-
menian Church, and to bequeath to it her melodic formulae
rather than scales, as well as the prose style and free rhythm
of her most ancient hymns.

Two principal Syrian rhythms to which the modes
were adjusted were:

Bar Hebraeus (1226-1286 of the Christian Era) says that
the early modes were used to describe the four qualities of
nature: cold, heat, dampness, and dryness. These modes
were often combined for variety and symbolic meaning,
so that eight modes came to be used regularly.[68]

68 Jeannin, J., *Mélodies Liturgiques Syriennes et Chaldéennes,* Chapter 1, page
   18. Also refer to Syrian modes in Appendix E, noting that each characteristically begins on an anacrusis.

CHAPTER VIII

ABYSSINIA:

LAND OF THE "TIGRITYA"

A DISTINCT AFFINITY OF CULTURE HAS ALWAYS EXISTED between Abyssinia and Palestine due, largely, to the fact that the royalty of Abyssinia has constantly asserted its direct descent from the royal house of Judah. Despite the fact that Abyssinia was later converted to Christianity, its church attempts to preserve the temple melodies which had been in use since early times.

Relatively little is known about Abyssinian arts generally, and scarcely any information is available concerning the type of music characteristic of Abyssinia in this early pre-Christian period. Mention of musical instruments is negligible, although we may presume that they borrowed

most of their instruments from their other Semitic neighbors. That their music was often an accompaniment to
parallelistic poetry or hymns can be ascertained by the
characteristic notation in texts calling for the shaking of
sistra at the end of each line. Polyphony existed, particularly in folk songs, and a complicated counterpoint was
used in vocal music. The *zafan* folk song was an excellent
example of this device; the soloist sang the verses and the
chorus joined in the refrain. All members would sing the
coda, which frequently was an overlapping repetition of
the melody, and the voices would drop out one by one
until only a single voice was left (similar to Haydn's
"Farewell Symphony").

The oldest form of instrumental counterpoint (at least
5000 years old), namely droning on double pipes, was a
characteristic of Abyssinian music, too. Resembling the
Egyptian method of droning, one pipe had its holes
stopped with wax or clay, permitting only one or two
tones to be played, while the other pipe, usually of higher
pitch, played the melody to the monotone accompaniment.

Abyssinian music appears to have been utilized chiefly
as accompaniment to the dance. We know of leaping lepers
who are said to have performed at sunrise before the doors
of those luckier than themselves. Instruments accompanied
these dancers, and possibly singing as well. Their melodies
were accompanied by a very simple harmony based on the
third. The most famous dance was the "Tigritya," which
was believed to be capable of exorcising devils and curing
the strange malady of "wasting away," apparently a common affliction among the Abyssinians. The ritual consisted
of a number of musicians playing very calm, soothing
music when first the sick one entered the room. The sub-

ject was settled and made comfortable, and the demon within him was then believed to have been lulled and soothed by the music. At this point, as the ailing person was on the verge of falling asleep, a group of men and women entered suddenly, whirling into a fast, maniacal dance, while the orchestra increased its volume sharply. If the sick one were truly possessed of an evil spirit, he would spring up and dance with the others, for demons are notoriously helpless to resist music. However, if the subject were not possessed of a devil, he would simply develop a headache and ask to leave the room.[68a]

Abyssinian musical instruments were, by and large, rather similar to those of their neighbors. Stringed instruments retained popularity, and included the *kessar*,[69] the

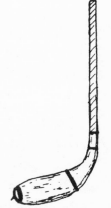

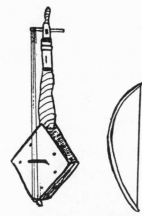

FIGURE T. ABYSSINIAN
TRUMPET (MALAKAT)

FIGURE U. ABYSSINIAN FIDDLE
WITH CRESCENT BOW

68a Engel, Carl, *Study in National Music,* Chapter 2.

69 An Abyssinian *kessar* was found, consisting of a square body, no sounding holes, ten strings on a wooden bridge five inches long by two and one half inches high, on which small pieces of leather were placed to separate the strings.

massaneqo fiddle with crescent-shaped bow (see Figure U), that which may have been the *bagana*, or standing lyre tuned pentatonically with a major third (Figure V), and a rather unusual bow-shaped lyre (Figure W). In Plate XXVIII, an Abyssinian *nagârit* or kettledrum appears, a descendant of the Uganda drum, its body of wood with the open ends covered with the hide of a white gemsbok, and laced with a series of twisted rawhide thongs. It contains a rattle inside and a smaller membrane for manipulating the tension of the larger one.

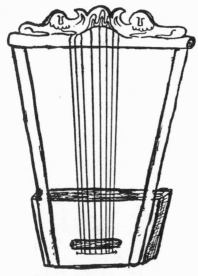

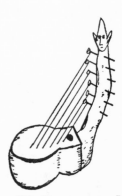

FIGURE V. ABYSSINIAN STANDING LYRE

FIGURE W. BOW-SHAPED LYRE

The Abyssinians developed a musical notation indicating that their music was far more highly evolved than we are able to judge. However, this system of notation was an elaborate and secret one, taught only to the initiated.

It consisted of syllables written above the sacred texts, and is explained by Sachs in his dissertation on Babylonian secret notation,[70] by comparing it with the notation of Abyssinian scripts. From his studies of the latter, he suggests that single syllables such as "he," "re," "me," "le," "se," probably indicate single or double tones, whereas double syllables, such as "lama," "raha", "rana," "rara," indicate group tones or grace notes. These frequently have been contracted into "hal," "las," "man," etc.[71] Although there are forty-seven different symbols in these sacred writings, they cover a wide field of musical expression including intervals, ascending and descending, dynamics, and intercalculated tones, such as grace notes and appoggiaturas.[72]

---

70 Sachs, Curt, "Mystery of Babylonian Notation," *Musical Quarterly*, Vol. XXVII, 1911, pp. 62-9.

71 Sachs, in *The Rise of Music in the Ancient World, East and West*, deals with a more complete description of this syllabic notation. He identifies such intervals as "se," indicating a descending semitone; "ka," an ascending whole tone; "wā," a whole tone with a trill on the higher note; "wa," a minor third; "we," an ascending fourth; "zeze," an ascending fifth; and "re," a final cadence.

72 See Appendix E for examples of Abyssinian music.

CONCLUSION

MUSIC, IN ANCIENT TIMES, PLAYED AN EXTREMELY IMPOR-
tant role in society; perhaps even a far more important
one in the daily life of the ancient peoples than it does in
our day-to-day living. One must not think of music in
early society as having been employed merely as a play-
thing to amuse the common people, or as a diversion for
the indulgence of kings, nobles, or of the royal harem.
Contrary to this, music was fully an integral part of the
lives of the people, an expression of everyday thoughts and
feelings, both sacred and secular, of man in the ancient
world. The fact that music, as such, was never restricted
to a particular class or stratum of society (except re-

ligiously, such as the Levites' elevation to the second highest post in the Temple worship), and that it was combined at all times with the other arts, particularly with dancing, recitation of poetry, and enactment of drama, demonstrates its vitality and spontaneity as an emotional folk art.

The definition of music given by Socrates, "the art that combines the playing of instruments with song and dance," expresses the very essence of ancient Near Eastern music. The Greeks derived the greater part of their music and perhaps other arts from that largely Semitic world with which they carried on trade and conquests. Certainly, the famous quotation of Plato, "Music is the general principle of human sciences—the gods have given it to us not only for the delight of the ear, but to establish harmony in the faculties of the soul," expresses specifically the aim and purpose of music received directly from Egypt, Palestine, and nearby cultures.

It is extremely difficult to evaluate the contribution of the Near Eastern peoples to world music for the following reasons: 1) we still lack accurate knowledge of the types of music employed at so early a period of human history; 2) we have been, thus far, only partly successful in deciphering texts and secret notations on the music of the particular era mentioned in this book; 3) thus far, we have uncovered no specific notation which will permit us to know precisely how the music of the ancient peoples sounded.

Nevertheless, we ought not to underrate the actual part played by the Near East in the history of the evolution of music. We may surmise that the following are some of the contributions due, in part if not completely, to the marvelous achievements of the ancient world:

a. Most modern instruments are the direct or indirect descendants of the instruments of the eight Near Eastern cultures mentioned herein.

b. The earliest known musical notations, while still not fully deciphered, can probably be traced back to Mesopotamia and Palestine. Particularly, we may consider the *trope* of the Old Testament as evidence of a workable notation predating the Latin neumes and later European notation.

c. The similarity of mode, patternization, intervallic structure, and flowing arhythmical style between the Temple music of the Hebrews and the Gregorian Chant, as well as the fact that the people representing both types received their religio-historical inception in the same environment, makes it apparent that the music of the Christian Church, as the most influential factor in Western music, owes much more than is commonly realized to the music of Palestine and the Temple.

d. The earliest known schools for the training and education of professional musicians existed in Egypt, Mesopotamia, and Palestine.

e. The possibility of polyphony as a European outgrowth of a Near Eastern development can be demonstrated in several ways. First, in the bas-reliefs, and paintings of ancient times, particularly those of Egypt, do we find portrayed harpists with instruments similar in size and tuning, but all plucking *different* strings. Since all of these works were executed with realistic, almost photographic accuracy, it is unthinkable that this single variation in a picture of uniform players could be accidental. Again we discover in a relief (now in the British Museum) representing the Elamite court orchestra welcoming the Assyrian conqueror (650 B.C.) performers, among whom are seated seven harpists plucking different strings, and producing (from Sach's analysis) an interval of a fifth. Secondly, we can recognize a very simple form of counterpoint, that of droning on pipes, to have existed as early as 5000 years ago in Sumeria and later in other nearby countries. With the popularity of antiphonal singing and accompaniment, it is conceivable that, in a natural way, the response gradually overlapped with the initial phrase sung or played, and thus canonic style was born.

f. Allusion has been made, from time to time, to the seven-tone scale employed by Egypt. It is conceivable that other cultures near Egypt, notably Palestine, employed the heptonic scale as well as the pentatonic. Indeed, there is no reason to believe that, although the pentatonic scale was favored, the heptonic scale could not have been known and used by all of the ancient Near Eastern peoples, since their destinies were obviously intertwined.

g. Not only style, modes, and scales were given to the Western world by the Near East, but several types of musical form owe their origin to the same source. Poetry was not the only art enriched by the dual parallelism popular in the ancient world, but undoubtedly this form helped to develop the phrase and period lengths in music. The motive was a core-idea which could be developed in any rambling fashion. But it was, without doubt, the balanced meter of parallelistic poetry which developed the motive into balanced phrase-lengths and period-lengths. Later, this reached a more highly evolved and varied plan in rondo form, a direct heritage of the Arabic *bashraw* form.

Perhaps, in the years to come, with the aid of newer

research, archaeologists and musicologists will make discoveries which will prove to us all the more how indebted
we are to the ancients. And, possibly, as the pendulum of
taste swings back and forth, the eagerness of scholars will
continue to forge ahead and to reveal anew the glories
of the past which have formed the bedrock of our present-
day culture. Perhaps, too, we shall continue to discover
valuable philosophies and concepts of the ancients, which,
in their eternal truth, can inspire our thought and further
our own development in the arts and in the growth of
civilization.

APPENDICES

APPENDIX A

Theoretical Notation of a Sumerian Hymn

Dr. E. Sievers analyzes Babylonian meter according to the "Schall-analyze" system, by attempting to recover the melodic intonation from the accentual stress of Sumerian or Akkadian words and their inflections. Thus, a rising sound is designated by /, a descending line by \, from high to low ∧, from low to high V, etc., etc. Galpin, in *Music of the Sumerians, Babylonians and Assyrians*, gives a translation of a hymn on the Creation of Man, of which a small section appears below, and analyzes it according to this method to derive the following possible musical notation for singer and harp accompaniment. The singer, probably in a fashion common to the East, ornamented his part freely with grace notes and slides on the descending intervals. Time-value is not given despite the quarter notes; merely melodic progression, for rhythm and stress depend upon the words.

A Hymn on the Creation of Man

When heav'n and earth, the constant pair, were fram'd	1
Divine Inanna, Mother Goddess, form'd;	2
When in the place ordain'd the earth was laid	3
And heav'n therewith in harmony design'd;	4
When, straight as line, stream and canal flow'd on	5
And Tigris and Euphrates fill'd their banks;	6
Then An and Enlil, Utu and Enki,	7
Gods almighty,	8
With the great gods, the Anunnaki,	9
Sat in their high abode majestical,	10
And one to another thus address'd their words:	11

113

SUMERIAN HYMN ON THE CREATION OF MAN

with harp accompaniment, of the second millennium B.C.

APPENDIX B

Egyptian Poetry

I SONG OF THE HARPER
   (*translated from the Harris Papyrus*)

O good prince, it is a decree,
That what hath been ordained thereby is well,
That the bodies of men shall pass away and disappear,
Whilst others remain.

Since the time of the oldest ancestors,
The gods who lived in olden times,
Who lie at rest in their sepulchres,
The Masters and also the Shining Ones,
Who have been buried in their splendid tombs,
Who have built sacrificial halls in their tombs,
Their place is no more.
Consider what hath become of them!

I have heard the words of Imhetep and Herutataf
Which are treasured above everything because they uttered them.
Consider what hath become of their tombs!
Their walls have been thrown down;
Their palaces are no more;
They are just as if they had never existed.

Not one of them cometh from where they are.
Who can describe to us their form,
Who can describe to us their surroundings.
Who can give comfort to our hearts
And act as our guide
To the place whereunto they have departed?

Give comfort to thy heart,
And let thy heart forget these things;
What is best for thee to do is
To follow thy heart's desire as long as thou livest.

Anoint thy head with sacred unguents,
Let thine apparel be of byssus
Dipped in costly perfumes,
In the veritable product of the gods.

Enjoy thyself more than thou hast ever done before,
And let not thy heart pine for lack of pleasure.

Pursue thy heart to desire and thine own happiness.
Order thy surroundings on earth in such a way
That they may minister to the desire of thy heart;
For at length that day of lamentation shall come,
Wherein he whose heart is still shall not hear the lamentation.

Never shall cries of grief cause
To beat again the heart of the man who is in the grave.
Therefore occupy thyself with thy pleasure daily,
And never cease to enjoy thyself.

Behold, a man is not permitted
To carry his possessions away with him.
Behold, there never was anyone who, having departed,
Was able to come back again.

II EGYPTIAN LOVE SONGS

Seven days from yesterday I have not seen my beloved,
And sickness hath crept over me,
And I am become heavy in my limbs,
And I am unmindful of mine own body.
If the master-physicians come to me,
My heart hath no comfort of their remedies,
And the magicians, no resources is in them,
My malady is not diagnosed.

Better for me is my beloved than any remedies,
More important is she for me than the entire compendium of
    medicine.
My salvation is when she enters from without,
When I see her then I am well;
Opens she her eye, my limbs are young again;
Speaks she and I am strong.
And when I embrace her she banishes evil,
And it passes from me for seven days.

         *   *   *   *   *

The little sycamore
Which she planted with her hand
She begins to speak,
And her words are as drops of honey,
She is charming, her bower is green—
She is laden with fruit
Redder than the ruby.
The color of her leaves is as glass,
Her stem is as the color of the opal . . .
It is cool in her shadow . . .
"Come spend this festival day,
And tomorrow, and the day after tomorrow,
Sitting in my shadow.
Thy companion sits at thy right hand . . .
And thou dost follow what he says . . .
I am of a silent nature,
And I do not tell what I see,
And I do not chatter."

III WISDOM POETRY
    (*Amenemope, Twenty-first Dynasty*)

Lay thee not down at night fearing the morrow;
When day dawns what is the morrow like?
Man knoweth not how the morrow may be.

God is ever efficient,
But man faileth ever,
The words that men say are one thing,
And the things that God doeth are another.

There is no success with God,
Nor is there failure before Him;
If a man turn him to seek success,
In a moment He destroyeth it.

Be resolute of heart, make firm thy mind,
Steer not with thy tongue;
The tongue of a man is the rudder of the boat,
But the Lord of all is its pilot.[73]

---

73 For more examples of Egyptian literature, refer to Budge, *Egyptian Literature.*

APPENDIX C
CHART of COMPARATIVE CANTILLATIONS
(From the Hebrew sources)

Ancient Form	Later Form	Hebrew Names	Oldest Latin Neumes
?	≈	Zarka (sprinkle)	
ϳ	⅃	Munach Shofar (resting horn)	⌐ Podatus
к	↗	Pazer (dispersed)	
∴		Segol	∴ Triangulata
⊽	⩒	Yerach ben Yomoh (young moon)	
⋊	⅍	Karne Farah (cow's horns)	⌣ Epiphonus
⋎	⅃	Kadmah V'azlah (preceding & going)	
⊢		Shilluk (cessation)	
⸪		Raviah (sustained)	• Punctum
⅂	⌐	Mapach Pashta (inverted horn)	
⑁	⅃⅃	Double Pashta	∖ Gravis
⸫		Munach or Zakeph Katon (minor rising)	⑃ Climacus
⌇		Shalsheleth (chain)	⋎ Quilisma
⫽	⅀	Gershayim (double geresh)	ⅉ Strophicus
⟋	⌐	Geresh (expulsion)	⟋ Virgula
⫽	⅌	Mercha Ch'fulah (two rods)	

Ancient Form	Later Form	Hebrew Names	Oldest Latin Neumes
ד	ﮋ	Darga (steps)	*s* Oriscus
ﮋ		T'vir (broken)	*ʒ* Salicos
﮳	ﮀ	Merche (lengthener)	
ﮮ	ﮮ	Tip'cha (handbreadth)	
ﮉ	ﮉ	Etnach'tah (rester)	∧ Clivis
ﮯ		Y'tiv (staying)	
﮲	﮲	T'lisha G'dolah (major drawing out)	
﮲	﮲	T'lisha K'tanah (drawing out)	

APPENDIX D

COMPARATIVE SCALES and METERS

SCALES [74]

I—Arabic	D, E, F, G, A, B, C, D
(tonal intervals	3/4 3/4 4/4 4/4 3/4 3/4 4/4
or steps)	
Greek Phrygian	D, E, F, G, A, B, C, D
	(minor characteristic)
	1 1/2 1 1 1 1/2 1

II—Arabic	E, F, G, A, B, C, D, E
	3/4 3/4 4/4 3/4 3/4 4/4 3/4
Dorian	E, F, G, A, B, C, D, E
	1/2 1 1 1 1/2 1 1

III—Arabic	F, G, A, B♭, C, D, E, F
	(major in character)
	4/4 4/4 2/4 4/4 4/4 3/4 3/4
Lydian	F, G, A, B♭, C, D, E, F
	1 1 1/2 1 1 1 1/2

IV—Arabic	D, E♭, F♯, G, A, B, C, D
	2/4 6/4 2/4 4/4 3/4 3/4 4/4
Hebrew	
Ahavah-Rabbah	D, E♭, F♯, G, A, B♭, C, D
	2/4 6/4 2/4 4/4 2/4 4/4 4/4

METERS [75]

1. Hazag   u - - ‿́ , u - - ‿́

2. Raǧaz   - - u ‿́ , - - u ‿́

---

(74) Idelsohn, *Jewish Music*, page 24.

(75) Idelsohn, *Gesänge der Orientalischen Sephardim*, page 13, Numbers 1, 2, 3, 4 and 8 quoted above are from this source.

3.	Mutákarib	u - ⏑́ , u - ⏑́ , u - ⏑́ , u - ⏑́
4.	Ramal	⏑́ u - - , ⏑́ u - - , ⏑́ u ⏑́ -
5.	Tawíl	- - ⏑́ , - - - - , - - ⏑́ , - - - -
6.	Saria	u ⏑́ ⏑́ u - , u - - , - u -
7.	Kamil	u u ⏑́ u , u u ⏑́ u , u u ⏑́ u -
8.	Basit	- - u - , - u -

APPENDIX E

MUSICAL EXAMPLES

PALESTINE

1. Shirat Hayyam (Song of Moses) from Idelsohn, *Jewish Music.*

2. Cadence of the Priestly Blessing.

3. Shofar Call (Jewish Encyclopedia)

(T'kiah)   (T'ruah)

(Sh'varim)   (T'kiah G'dolah)

4. Traditional Music from Alexandrian Synagogue.

5. Song of Yemenite Women (from Gradenwitz, *Music of Israel*).

Two women sing, accompanying themselves with frame-drum and cymbals.
This is repeated seven times.

6. Hymn of Moroccan Jews.

7. Hymn of Moroccan Jews, containing Oriental scale technique similar to the twelve-tone system; exposition of the "series", variation and modification of the original "theme". From E. Gerson-Kiwi.

First phrase   Second phrase

Third phrase not quoted   Fourth phrase   etc.

Fifth phrase

ARABIA

1. Song of the Water-Carriers of Mecca.   2. Ramadan Song of Palestinian Araba. (solo)

castanets ... etc.

(chorus)   (solo)

(instrumental interlude)

(chorus)

3. Algerian Women's Song.   (accom. by clapping)   (inst. interl.)

4. Prayer Call from Oulad Yanez (Thompson's Cyclopedia)

ARABIAN MODES (from Idelsohn)

1. Bayati

3. Siga

4. Sasgar

5. Ağam

Sabba
Scale   3/4   3/4   2/4   6/4 2/4 1   2/4   5/4   3/4

Allahu Akbar (Hejaz mode) - from Idelsohn.

COMPARATIVE TABLE OF ACCENT MOTIVES OF THE PENTATEUCH   (after
Idelsohn - Gerschichte der Babylonischen Juden,
p. 44)

SYRIA
Modes from Jeannin, <u>Melodies Liturgiques</u>.

9. presto

10. allegro

11. andante

ABYSSINIA
(from Sachs)

BIBLIOGRAPHY

ALBRIGHT, WILLIAM FOXWELL. *The Archaeology of Palestine.* London, 1949.

——. *From the Stone Age to Christianity.* Baltimore, 1946.

BAIKIE, JAMES. *The Story of the Pharaohs.* London, 1908.

BREASTED, JAMES HENRY. *The Conquest of Civilization.* New York, 1926.

——. *Ancient Times, a History of the Early World,* Boston, 1916.

——. *Egypt through the Stereoscope.* New York, 1905.

BUDGE, ERNEST A. WALLIS. *Literature of the Ancient Egyptians.* London, 1914.

—— (ed.). *Annals of the Kings of Assyria.* London, 1902.

——. *Egyptian Tales and Romances.* London 1931.

——. *Babylonian Life and History.* London, 1886.

BURROWS, MILLAR. *What Mean These Stones?* New Haven, 1941.

CAPART, JEAN. *Primitive Art in Egypt.* Philadelphia, 1905.

CERAM, C. W. *Gods, Graves and Scholars.* New York, 1951.

CONTENAU, G. *La Civilisation Phénicienne.* Paris, 1949.

DAVIES AND GARDINER. *Ancient Egyptian Paintings.* Vol. 1, 2, Chicago, 1949.

DELAPORTE, LOUIS. *La Mesopotamie: Les civilisations Babylonienne et Assyrienne.* Paris, 1923.

D'ERLANGER, RODOLPHE. *La Musique Arabe.* Paris, 1935-49.

EDGERLY, BEATRICE. *From the Hunter's Bow.* New York, 1942.

ENGEL, CARL. *Musical Instruments.* London, 1875.

——. *Music of the Most Ancient Nations.* London, 1909.

——. *Introduction to the Study of National Music.* London, 1866.

ERMAN, ADOLF. *Life in Ancient Egypt.* London, 1894.

——. *Literature of the Ancient Egyptians.* New York, 1927.

EWEN, DAVID. *Hebrew Music.* New York, 1931.

FARMER-DANIEL, F. S. *Music and Musical Instruments of the Arabs.* London, 1915.

FARMER, HENRY GEORGE. *The Organ of the Ancients from Eastern Sources.* London, 1931.

FINEGAN, JACK. *Light from the Ancient Past.* New York, 1945.

GALPIN, FRANCIS W. *Music of the Sumerians.* Cambridge, 1937.

GASTER, THEODORE H. *Oldest Stories in the World.* New York, 1952.

GERSON-KIWI, EDITH. *Music of the Orient, Ancient and Modern.* Tel Aviv, 1949.

GLANVILLE, S. R. K. *Legacy of Egypt.* Oxford, 1943.

GLUECK, NELSON. *The River Jordan.* Philadelphia, 1946.

GOLDMAN, SOLOMON (ed.). *The Book of Books.* New York, 1948.

GORDON, CYRUS H. *The Living Past.* New York, 1941.

GRADENWITZ, PETER. *Music of Israel.* New York, 1949.

HALL, H. R. *Ancient History of the Near East.* London, 1936.

HEIDEL, ALEXANDER. *Gilgamesh Epic and Old Testament Parallels.* Chicago, 1946.

HITTI, PHILIP K. *History of Syria.* New York, 1951.

———. *The Arabs.* Princeton, 1949.

HUTCHINSON, ENOCH. *Music of the Bible.* Boston, 1864.

IDELSOHN, ABRAHAM Z. *Thesaurus:* Berlin, 1923.
"Gesänge der Orientalischen Sephardim"
"Gesänge der Marokkanischen Juden"
"Gesänge der Babylonischen Juden"
"Gesänge der Jemenitischen Juden"

———. *Jewish Liturgy and Its Development.* New York, 1932.

———. *Jewish Music and Its Historical Development.* New York, 1929.

JASTROW, MORRIS, JR. *Civilizations of Babylonia and Assyria.* Philadelphia, 1915.

JEANNIN, JULES. *Mélodies Liturgiques Syriennes et Chaldéennes.* Paris, 1924.

JOSEPHUS, FLAVIUS. *Antiquities* VII, XII, (ed.) Hudson, London, 1733.

KRAMER, SAMUEL NOAH. *Enki and Ninhursag.* New Haven, 1945.

———. *Gilgamesh and the Huluppu Tree.* Chicago, 1938.

———. *Lamentations over the Destruction of Ur.* Chicago, 1940.

———. *Sumerian Mythology.* Philadelphia, 1949.

LANG, PAUL HENRY. *Music in Western Civilization.* New York, 1941.

LANGDON, STEPHEN HERBERT. *Sumerian and Babylonian Psalms.* New York, 1909.

LEGRAIN, LEON. *Culture of the Babylonians.* (Babylonian Section, University Museum) Vol. XIV, Philadelphia, 1925.

LESLAU, WOLF. *Falasha Anthology*. Yale University Press, 1951.

MASPERO, GASTON C. C. *Dawn of Civilization in Egypt and Chaldea*. London, 1897.

MYHRMAN, DAVID W. *Babylonian Hymns and Prayers*. Philadelphia, 1911.

OESTERLEY AND ROBINSON. *History of Israel*. Oxford, 1932.

OESTERLEY, WILLIAM O. E. *Jewish Background of Christian Liturgy*. Oxford, 1925.

O'LEARY, DELACY. *Arabia before Muhammed*. New York, 1927.

OLMSTEAD, ALBERT TEN EYCK. *History of Palestine and Syria*. New York, 1931.

PERROT, G. and CHIPIEZ, C. *History of Art in Phoenicia and its Dependencies*. London, 1885.

———. *History of Art in Chaldea and Assyria*. London, 1884.

———. *History of Art in Ancient Egypt*. London, 1883.

PHILO JUDAEUS. *About the Contemplative Life*. Oxford, 1895.

PRATT, WALDO SELDEN. *History of Music*. New York, 1907.

RAWLINSON, GEORGE. *History of Phoenicia*. New York, 1889.

REIFENBERG, A. *Ancient Hebrew Arts*. New York, 1950.

RIEMANN, HUGO. *Geschichte der Musiktheorie im IX-XIX Jahrhundert*. Berlin, 1920.

ROSS, EDWARD DENISON. *Art of Egypt through the Ages*. New York, 1931.

ROTH, CECIL. *Short History of the Jewish People*. London, 1936.

SACHS, CURT. *The Rise of Music in the Ancient World, East and West*. New York, 1943.

———. *The Commonwealth of Art*. New York, 1946.

———. *Die Musikinstrumente des Alten Ægyptens*. Berlin, 1913.

———. *History of Musical Instruments*. New York, 1940.

———. *World History of the Dance*. New York, 1937.

SAMINSKY, LAZAR. *Music of the Ghetto and Bible*. New York, 1934.

SCHAEFER, H. and ANDRAE, W. *Die Kunst des Alten Orients*. Berlin, 1925.

SCHAEFFNER, ANDRÉ. *Origine des Instruments de Musique*. Paris, 1936.

SMITH, HERMANN. *The World's Earliest Music*. London 18—.

STAINER, SIR JOHN. *Music of the Bible*. London, 1879.

STEINDORFF, G. and SEELE, K. *When Egypt Ruled the East*. Chicago, 1942.

STEINDORFF, GEORG. *Die Kunst der Ægypter*. Leipzig, 1928.

TYLOR, SIR EDWARD. *Anthropology—Introduction to the Study of Man and Civilization.* New Haven, 1898.

WILEY, LULU RUMSEY. *Bible Music.* New York, 1945.

WILKINSON, SIR JOHN GARDNER. *Manners and Customs of the Ancient Egyptians.* London, 1878.

WOOLEY, SIR C. LEONARD. *Ur Excavations from the Royal Cemetery,* Vol. 2, London, 1929.

———. *Development of Sumerian Art.* New York, 1935.

The Bible, Old Testament. Jewish Publication Society Version: Ezra 2:65; 2:45; Nehemiah 7:67; I Chronicles 15:16; 25; Numbers 10; Daniel 3:10. II Chronicles 5:12; 7; Joshua 14; 33.

The Babylonian Talmud. Shekalim 5:1; Yomah 3:11; Arukin 2:3; Tamid 7:3-4; Kelim; Agadah; Sukkah 50, 51.

Cambridge, Ancient History. Vol. 3, "The Assyrian Empire," New York, 1923-27.

Encyclopedia Americana. Vol. 3, p. 645, 612, 624; Vol. 14, p. 57; Vol. 19, pp. 124-145.

Grand Dictionnaire Universel. XIXe siècle.

Grove's Dictionary of Music and Musicians. Ed. Colles, New York, 1927. (See all Semitic references.)

Macmillan Encyclopedia of Music and Musicians. Ed. Weir, New York, 1938.

New International Encyclopedia. Vol. 16, p. 479; Vol. 11, p. 75.

SCHOLES, PERCY A. *Oxford Companion to Music,* New York, 1950.

THOMPSON, OSCAR. *International Cyclopedia of Music and Musicians.* 5th ed., New York, 1949.

Universal Jewish Encyclopedia. Vol. 11, p. 365; Vol. 8, p. 46.

Biblical Archeology. 1941, Sellers, "Musical Instruments of Israel."

Hebrew Union College Annual. Vol. 26, Werner and Sonne, "Philosophy and Theory of Music in Judeo-Arabic Literature."
1926 vol., Finesinger, "Musical Instruments of the Old Testament."

L'Institut Français d'Archéologie Orientale. Caire, 1946, Hickmann, Hans, "La Trompette dans l'Egypte Ancienne."

Revue de Musicologie. Juillet, 1950, article by Hickmann.

HICKMANN, HANS, "Classement et classification des flûtes, clarinettes et hautbois de l'Egypte ancienne."

HICKMANN, HANS, "La Cliquette, un instrument de percussion Egyptien de l'époque copte."

HICKMANN, HANS, "Zur Geschichte der altägyptischen Glocken."

Die Musik in Geschichte und Gegenwart. Hickman, Hans, "Ægyptische Musik" "Æthiopische Musik"

Die Musikforschung. Article by Hans Hickmann.

Miscellanea Musicologica. Hickmann, Hans, "Les Harpes de la Tombe de Ramsès III."

Hickmann, Hans, "Le Tambourin Rectangulaire du Nouvel Empire."

Metropolitan Museum, New York, Handbook no. 13. Catalogue of musical instruments of all nations.

Musical Quarterly. Vol. 27, 1941, pp. 62-69, Sachs, Curt, "Mystery of Babylonian Notation."

Musical Times. Oct. 1, 1890, "Recent Discovery of Egyptian Flutes and Their Significance."

Musical Times. Dec. 1, 1890, "Egyptian Flutes."

Musical Times. Dec. 1, 1915, "Israel's Music Lesson in Egypt."

National Geographic Magazine. Jan. 1951, pp. 41-105, Speiser, "Ancient Mesopotamia, A Light That Did Not Fail."

Proceedings of the American Academy of Jewish Research. 1947, Werner, "Oldest Sources of Synagogual Chant."

Proceedings American Philosophical Society. 1942, Kramer, Samuel N., "Sumerian Literature: Preliminary Survey of the Oldest Literature in the World."

Internationale Musik-Geselschaft Sammelbänder. Vol. 2, p. 167, Schlesinger, Kathleen, "Researches into the Origin of the Organs of the Ancients."

University Museum Publications. Philadelphia. (See all Semitic references.)

University of Chicago, Oriental Institute Publications. "Mastaba of Mereruka." Vol. 39, Part 1 and 2.

INDEX

A

Abraham, 49, 51, 52
Abyssinia, 103-107
  music of, Appendix E
  musical development, 104, 106, 107
  musical instruments, 105
Accent motives, 126
Adam, v, 53
African tribes, xx, 22
Akkadians, 2, 3, 4, 5, 6, 14, 15, 86,113
Amarna, 36, 50, 51, 100
  (see also Tel-el-Amarna)
Antiphony, 57, 71, 75, 76, 111
Arabia, 77-85
  art and religion, 78
  early life and customs, 77, 78
  music of, 79-83, Appendix E
  musical instruments, 78, 79-83, Figures J, K, L, Plates XVII, XXI, XXIII, XXIV, XXV, XXVI
  musical systems, 83-85, Appendices D, E
  musical usage, 83-85
Archaeology, v, vi, 50, 51
Art (see specific country)
Assur, 86
Assyria, 86-94, 95, 110, 111
  art, 87, 88
  life, 87
  literature, 89
  music of, 89-94

B

Babylonia, 1, 3, 12, 14, 20, 36, 67, 68, 95, 126
Bagpipe, 62, 63, 66, 80, 91, 101, Figure J, Plate XVI
Bells, 16, 32, 38, 55, 60, 79, 90, 101

Beni Hasan, x, 26, 68
Bezalel, 52
Bible lands (see map)
Biblical characters (see David, Saul, etc.)
Bow, xx, 42, 105, Figures A, U
Bullroarer, 37, Figure E

C

Cain, daughter of, 78
Cantillations, 73, 74, Appendix C
Castanets, 32, 34, 38, 90, 101
Chamber orchestras, 47, 59, Plates XI, XII
Chants, primitive, xvii
Cithara, 19, 53, 56, 67, 70, Plate X
Clappers, 16, 34, 36, 37, 42, 60
Clarinet, 41, Plate XIII
Clavichord, 82
Cleopatra, 33
Concussion sticks, 16, 36, Plate III
Counterpoint (see Polyphony)
Cuneiform, x
Cylinder Seals, x
Cymbals, 16, 32, 38, 58-60, 72, 90, 97, 101, Figure M, Plate XIX

D

Dance, xvii, xx, xxi, 21, 31-34, 37, 45, 57, 104, Plate III
David, 53, 56, 57, 58, 60, 69
Drums, xix, 15, 16, 21, 36, 39, 42, 46, 60, 78, 79, 90, 93, 97, 100, 101, 106, Figures C, S, Plate XXVIII
Dulcimer, 69, 82, 92, Plate IX

E

Egypt, ix, x, xx, 6, 16, 22-48, 54, 74, 75, 85, 89, 94, 95, 96, 99, 104, 109, 110
  architecture, 28

art,   24, 26-33
dance,   31-34, 37
early life and customs,   22, 23,
                                        25, 30, 32
literature, 26, 28, 29, Appendix B
music,   24, 31-36, 46-48
musical instruments,   16, 24, 31,
    32, 33, 34-46, Figures G, H,
        Plates XI, XII, XIII, XX
Enlil,   20
Erech,   7, 9, 20
Ezion-Geber,   52

F

Fara,   16
Fiddle,   106, Figure U
                  (see also Lute, etc.)
Flageolet,   61, Plate XV
Flute, xix, 16, 17, 32, 35, 36, 39-41,
    46, 47-48, 61-62, 70, 79, 80,
    90-91, 97, 100, Figures F, N,
                   O, R, Plate XIV
Flute-à-bec,   xx
Funeral,   30, 43, 62

G

Gilgamesh,   7, 8, 12, 13, 18, 21,
                              Plate II
Gong,   xix
Greeks,   v, ix, xx, 5, 6, 27, 36,
        67, 84, 95, 109, 121
Gudea,   4, 16, 17, 21
Guitar,   60, 67

H

Hamito-Semitic,   22
Hammurabi,   ix, 2, 6
Harp,   xx, 12, 18, 20, 24, 30, 32,
    33, 35, 36, 42, 43, 44, 47, 48,
    53, 55, 56, 57, 58, 59, 67, 69,
    72, 73, 83, 92, 93, 98, 110,
    111, Figures H, P, Plates I,
                         II, IX, XI
Hebrews, ix, 5, 6, 30, 49-76, 97, 110
    architecture,   51, 52
    art,   52
    Bible,   49
    dance,   57
    early life and customs,   51, 52
    idioms,   ix

music of,   Appendices C, D, E
musical development, 53-58, 72-75
musical instruments,   59-70
names,   ix
Hezekiah,   52, 57
Hieroglyphics,   27
Hittite,   3, 51
Horn,   xix, xx, 17, 53, 64, 91, 92
            Plates XVIII, XIX, XXII
Hydraulis,   64, Plate XVII
Hyksos,   24, 54

I

Innini,   20
Instruments, primitive,   xix
    (see also specific type and
    country)
Intervals,   xviii, xix, 110

J

Jacob,   54
Joseph,   25, 26
Jubal,   53, 54, 78

K

Kaina,   79
Kanoon,   79, 82, 84, Figure K
Karan,   18
Kemângeh-a-gûz, 81, 82, Plate XXV
Kessar,   82, 83, 105, Figure L
Kish,   7, 16
Kouyunjik,   89, 100

L

Lady Maket,   48
Lady Shubad,   18
Lagash,   1, 16
Levites,   58, 59, 72, 109
Libyan tribes,   22
Lute,   20, 24, 33, 36, 45, 46, 55,
    69, 78, 79, 81, 83, 92, 99, 100,
    Plates VIII, XI, XXIII, XXIV
Lyre,   18, 19, 20, 32, 33, 36, 44,
    45, 47, 48, 53, 59, 67, 68, 72,
    79, 83, 92, 93, 98, 99, 100, 106,
    Figures G, L, Q, V, W, Plates
                         XI, XX

M

Mandolin,   xx, 81

Map,   Plate section XXIX
Mesopotamia,   x, 1-21, 85, 94, 110
    architecture,   4
    art,   3, 4
    early life and customs,   1-6
    literature,   5-14
    music of,   Appendix A
    musical instruments,   15-20,
                    Figure C, Plates I-X
    musical systems,   15-16
Meters,   Appendix D
Miriam,   55, 60
Mohammed,   78
Moses,   52, 53, 76
Musical instruments
    (see Bells, Flute, etc.)
Musical systems,   xx
    (see also Egypt, Mesopotamia,
    etc.)

                    N
Naram-Sin,   21
Nebuchadnezzar,   4
Nefretiti,   viii, 25
Nippur,   4, 6, 8, 9
Nuzu,   50
Notation
    secret,   14, 107
    theoretical,   Appendix A

                    O
Obelisk,   26, 87
Oboe,   17, 33, 34, 36, 41, 46, 58,
       59, 61, 62, 79, 80, 91, Plates
       IV, V, VI, XI, XII
Odyssey,   xx
Oliphant,   66, Plate XIX
Orchestra,   32, 33, 45, 47, 93,
                        Plates XI, XII
Organ,   62, 63, 79, 83, 85,
                          Plate XVII

                    P
Palestine,   viii, x, 36, 49-76, 85,
           89, 95, 96, 103, 109, 110
    (see also Hebrews)
Percussives
    (see Bells, Drums, etc.)
Persia,   viii, 33, 49, 72, 81, 94
Phoenicia,   36, 88, 95-98

art,   96
life,   95, 96
music of,   96, 97
musical instruments,   97, 98,
                             Figure R
Piano,   82
Pipe(s),   17, 24, 47, 53, 61, 62,
       70, 91, 93, 97, 100, 104, Figures
       O, R (see also Flute, Flageo-
       let, etc.)
Plato,   109
"Poem of Creation,"   1, 7
Poetry,   xviii
    (see specific country)
Polyphony,   xviii, 71, 104
Psalms,   56, 70, 71, 72, 73, 74, 75
Psalter(y),   53, 57, 69, 82, 83, 97,
                             Figure R
Pyramid,   23, 24, 26, 29

                    R
Rattle,   xix, 16
Rebâb,   81, 82, Plate XXVI
Romans,   ix, xx

                    S
Sambuc(c)a,   67, 93, 100
Santir,   82, 93
Sargon,   2, 21, 36, 87
Scales,   xx, 47, 83, 84, 111,
                          Appendix D
Semites, v, vi, viii, ix, 2, 14, 17, 70
Shamash,   20
Sheba, Queen of,   57
Shiloh tunnel,   52
Shofar,   64-66, 123
Singing,   xvii, xviii, 18, 21, 30, 31,
       32, 33, 34, 35, 53, 56, 57, 58,
       59, 71, 72, 93, 100
Sinauhe,   25
Sippar,   20
Sistrum,   16, 32, 37, 38, 46, 57,
              58, 59, 69, Figure D
Socrates,   109
Song,   31, 32, 33, 46, 47,
                        78, 83, 84, 85
"Song of the Harper,"   25
"Song of Songs,"   viii, 74
Solomon,   52, 55, 56, 57, 58, 96
Source materials,   x, xi, 74

Spinet, 82
Stringed instruments
Egyptian, 43, Figure G
(see also Lute, Lyre, etc.)
Sumerians, vi, viii, 2, 3, 4, 5, 7,
14, 15, 60, 86, 113
Syria, 33, 36, 54, 68, 99-102
music of, Appendix E
musical development, 101, 102
musical instruments, 100, 101

T
Talmud, 58, 59, 60, 61, 62, 63, 65,
66, 69, 72, 73
Tamboura, 32, 45, 92, 100
Tambourine, 32, 39, 60, 78, 79,
Plate XXI
Tel-el-Amarna, 6, 50, 51
(see also Amarna)
Temple at Jerusalem, 55, 56, 57,
58, 59, 62, 64, 65, 67, 70,
72, 76, 77, 96
Thebes, 35
Timbrel, 55, 60, 97, 98, Figure R
Trombone, 66

Trope, 73
Trumpet, 17, 40, 41, 42, 53, 57,
58, 66, 72, 79, 80, 91, 101, 105,
Figures F, T, Plates XXII,
XXVII

U
Ugaritic texts, 50
Ur, 1, 2, 9, 15, 17, 18

W
Wedding music, 62, 94
Whistle, xvii, xix, xx, 62,
Figure B
Wind instruments
(see Flute, Shofar, etc.)

Y
Yemen, 72, 73, Appendix E

Z
Zither, 58, 69, 82, 92, 97
Zulus, xix, xx
Zumarah, 16